Beginner's Guide to the Obsidian Note Taking App and Second Brain

Everything you Need to Know About the Obsidian Software with 70+ Screenshots to Guide you

© Marc A. Palmer

Marc A. Palmer

Beginner's Guide to the

Obsidian

Note Taking App and Second Brain

Everything you Need to Know About the Obsidian Software

with 70+ Screenshots

to Guide you

ISBN 978-3-3060-2583-0

Creafe Publishing

All rights reserved.

Copyright © by Marc A. Palmer, 2023

Table of Contents

Table of Contents 5
   Introduction 9
   What is Obsidian? 10
   So why Markdown in the first place? 11
   Why use Obsidian App 11
   Obsidian Sync 12
   Mobile Apps 12
Getting Started 13
   Interface 16
      Toolbar 17
      Files/Folders Section 17
      Active document 17
      Links Directory 17
      Left-Most Panel (Top Left) 19
      Settings 27
      Important Core Plug-ins to use in your Obsidian 35
      How to Name Notes with Zettelkasten prefixer core plug-in in Obsidian 39
   Shortcuts / Basic Formatting 44
      Convert to Reading Mode 44
      Command Palette 44
      Create New Note 44
      Close Window 45
      Switch Between Notes 45
      Creating New Internal Links 45
      Numbered or Bullet Point while making a list 45
      For headings 45
      Changing font in Obsidian 45

Adding Footnotes 46
Creating Table on Obsidian 47
To Bold Texts 47
Quotation 47
Horizontal Line Split 47
Hyperlink 48
Graph View 48
Opens Quick Switcher (File Browser) 48
Edit Mode/ View Mode Toggle 48
Strikethrough text 48
Highlighting Text 48
Underlining Text 48
Code blocks 49
Adding checklist 49

Choosing a Theme 50

Setting Up Your Folders 51

Creating your First Note 52

Organizing Notes 57

How to search for text in a note 58
Using Note Dates for Quick Search 59
Note Search with Tags 60
Searching for To-do items 61

Common Obsidian Styles 63
Editor Mode 63
Research Mode 64
Clean Writer 64
A/B Mode 65

Text Editing 66

Split View 68
Why is a split view important? 69

How to Import Files 70
Importing Images 70

    Drag the image into the note interface 70

    Use Markdown syntax 71

  Importing Audio and Videos 71

  Importing PDFs 72

Knowledge Graph 73

  Graph View Details 75

  Drilling down 76

  Filters 76

  Common Filters 77

    Search 77

    Standard Toggles 77

    Global Graph Extras 77

    Local Graph Extras 78

    External and Internal Links 78

    Interlinks 78

    Display 78

    Forces 79

Using YAML in your Obsidian App 80

How to embed pages in Obsidian? 81

Queries and Search 82

Links, Tags, and Backlinks 83

  Internal Links 83

  Backlinks 85

  Tags 87

Scanning documents into Obsidian 88

  Step 1: Adjust the configuration 88

  Step 2: Save 89

  Step 3: Choose file options 90

  Step 4: Making a Note on the PDF 91

How to Secure your Ideas and Notes in Obsidian 92

  Securing physical data access on Obsidian 92

  Securing digital data access on Obsidian 93

    Data encoding..94
        Notes syncing and cloud security..95
    How to secure Obsidian on mobile devices 95
        Extra Safety Tips 96
Best Practices 97
    Record Often 97
    Review meticulously...97
Conclusion 98

Introduction

Keeping track of ideas requires more than just a notepad; you need a system that can help network between those ideas to create highly relatable and rational thoughts just like the Brain.

Fortunately, we are at the tech stage where options are available to connect our ideas and bring our dreams to light. This concept is the Brain behind the development of [Obsidian](#) to help create a flexible note management system for both personal and commercial use.

Currently, many note-taking programs are available, and chances are you are already using one.

So why is it worthwhile for you to migrate to Obsidian?

Is it not just one of those regular note-taking apps?

How is it any better? What are the benefits, and why should you care?

As we will see in this book, there are so many features that clearly distinguish the Obsidian, and quite obvious that the details in this guide will serve as a warranty. But before we continue, we will need to understand what Obsidian is and what makes it different.

What is Obsidian?

Obsidian is a unique and highly effective knowledge management app. It's built as a "second brain," a markdown-based file reader with tags, plug-ins, and backlinks that can be linked to any relevant files in a designated folder or Vault to enable users to write, edit and interlink their notes. Your notes are kept locally and remotely utilizing iCloud, GitHub, Google Drive, and others.

Markdown is an internet-based system (HTML) designed to stand the test of time.

Originally launched in 2020 by Erica Xu and Shida Li, Obsidian reduces the risk of losing ideas and notes and saves you from any compatibility issues and data loss in the foreseeable future, free of charge.

Yeah, all for free! (Personal use)

By making it free for personal use, Obsidian has eliminated the issue of experimentation. It also does not need you to log in or sign up for anything. This implies that your personal information won't be shared or sold without your consent.

As stated earlier, Obsidian uses Markdown files instead of conventional note-taking formats, which has the significant benefit of making any personal idea future-proof. Your notes can be transferred to another editor, and you can easily search and open them in plain text. If you switch from Windows to Mac or Linux, there won't be any issues.

With this App, you can create a personal wiki, which most distinguishes it from traditional note-taking systems. This powerful tool is suited for a while range of professional fields and is an ultimate must-have for anyone serious about knowledge management. However, if you're a student, professional writer, blogger, designer, programmer, or researcher, it's an excellent choice because it gives full flexibility and customization control over the notes without any monthly subscription fee.

As a networked note-taking tool, it operates on the principle of bi-directional (backlink) connection, which makes taking notes incredibly simple. Networked notetaking is the scientifically supported premise that creative ideas emerge when they are recorded and given the freedom to engage in a networked context freely.

Obsidian simulates the brain's search for arbitrary links across stored memories. However, building a concept involves treating each note as a separate repository of thought and then connecting it to other related thoughts. Because of its ability to generate highly comprehensible connections, Obsidian can help identify patterns in your notes, which makes it easy to see how some of your notes relate to one another in unexpected ways, thanks to those patterns. With this, you just created for yourself a highly effective "second brain" with total ease.

Your Obsidian notes are stored locally on your Mac or Windows PC. Few people are aware of the implication of cloud storage, mobile app-based workflows, and the web ecosystem as it grows in popularity. And that isn't good, especially with regard to delicate information like blueprints and prototype concepts.

With a highly effective system, you can install your Obsidian App on Mac, Windows, and Linux as a desktop application.

Obsidian currently has a community of about 70,000 active members on Discord and 35,000 on the forum worldwide. So, it is easy to get answers to any question you may have. The best part is you do not have constraints with language as Obsidian App is translated into about 22 languages, with more translations expected soon. So, you can build a huge community of like-minded people.

So why Markdown in the first place?

The markdown work concept allows Obsidian to easily write codes without switching contexts between note-taking applications or even IDEs. But does being a markdown-based application make it a preferred choice? Why should I even consider it? Here are some of the reasons why Markdown is worth a trial:

- Simple and Easy to Use
- Bridges the gap between coding and plain text writing
- You can quickly take notes and write some code using Markdown without
- Conveniently, employ headers, checkboxes, tables, lists, and web links with simple syntax.

Why use Obsidian App

- Compatibility with a wide range of platforms
- Free and instant
- Fantastic tool for writers to concentrate with a modest word count
- Add and view files, such as Images, PDFs, and audio files
- View relationships between notes and objects in graph view.
- References current note in other notes
- Active community that is willing to help anytime

Obsidian Sync

Obsidian offers a paid, premium, encrypted sync option, which automatically keeps files in sync on mobile devices. Premium Obsidian Sync isn't required; it is the most comprehensive option for keeping vaults synced across desktop and mobile devices. There's an annual fee for commercial use, and they also offer a "Catalyst" tier for Obsidian enthusiasts to support the team and get early access to new features. However, you don't need to pay anything if you use it for notetaking and creativity.

Mobile Apps

Obsidian also offers mobile apps, available for iOS and Android, so that you can access your knowledge management system while you don't have access to your computer. The iOS version works on both iPhone and iPad.

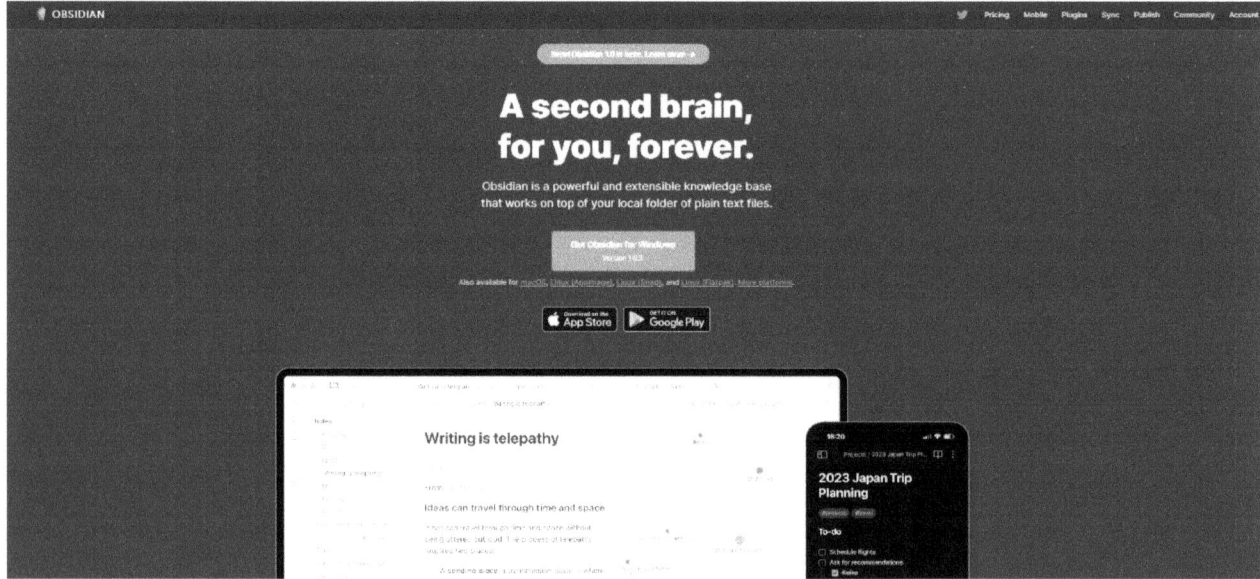

However, the core reason for compiling this beginner's guide is to give step-by-step, in-depth procedures to use Obsidian for optimal productivity. Now that you know what Obsidian is and what to expect let's start with the fundamentals.

Getting Started

Even though using Obsidian can be daunting at first, it isn't rocket science and can certainly be done with little ease. If you follow the processes stated in this guide, you can conveniently use the App to enhance your personal and career life while increasing productivity. So, before we start with details, the first step is to install a version compatible with your Operating System (Windows, Linux, or Mac), download and start using it. We will go through the steps soon, but the best part is that you can use Obsidian on your mobile phone as well, click here if you are an iPhone user to install via the App Store or here for Android Smartphone users. To install it on your computer, click here to initiate installation. Once done, you will see the screen below:

After installation, you will need to create a vault. It is a folder that stores your notes in the local file system; it can also be linked to **Dropbox**. However, your note can be in separate vaults or one single Vault.

Then select "Create new Vault" and follow the instruction that will redirect you to the location in the computer, then choose where to save the notes.

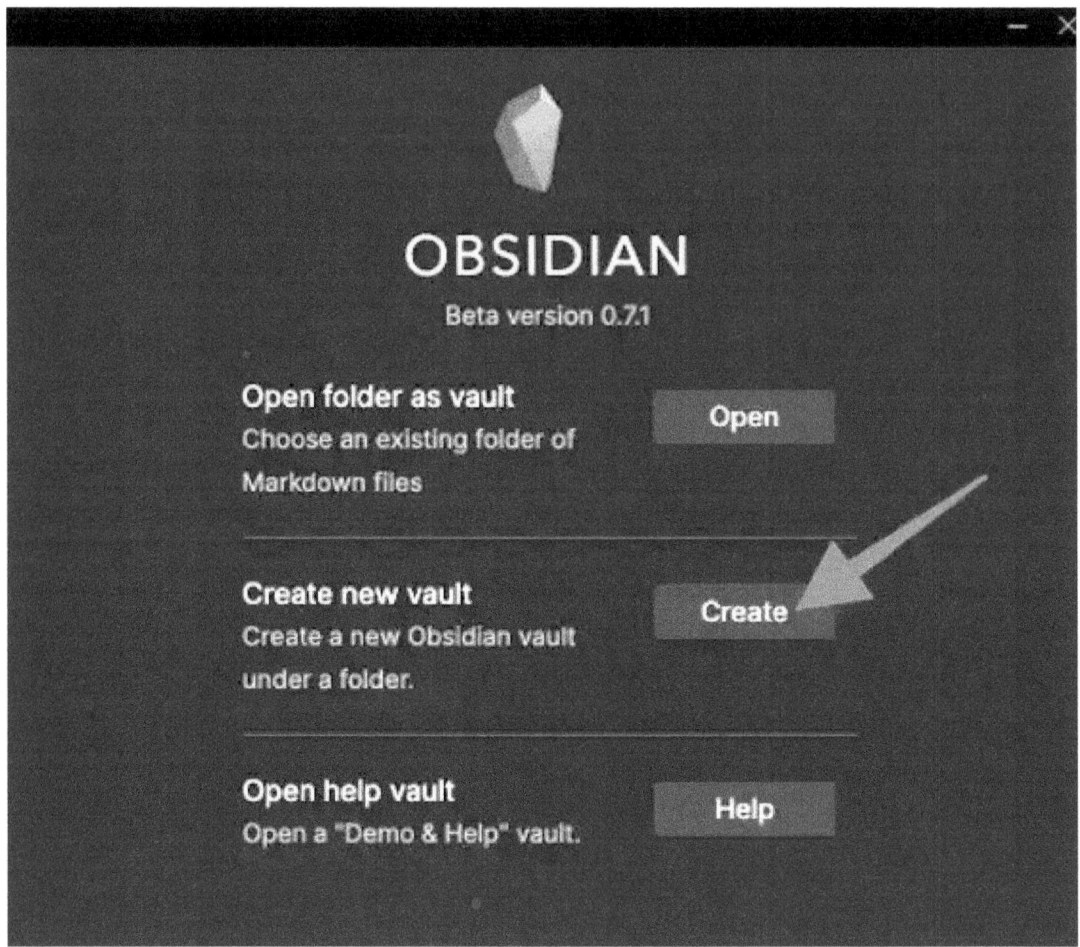

Change the vault name if you want and click on **Create**.

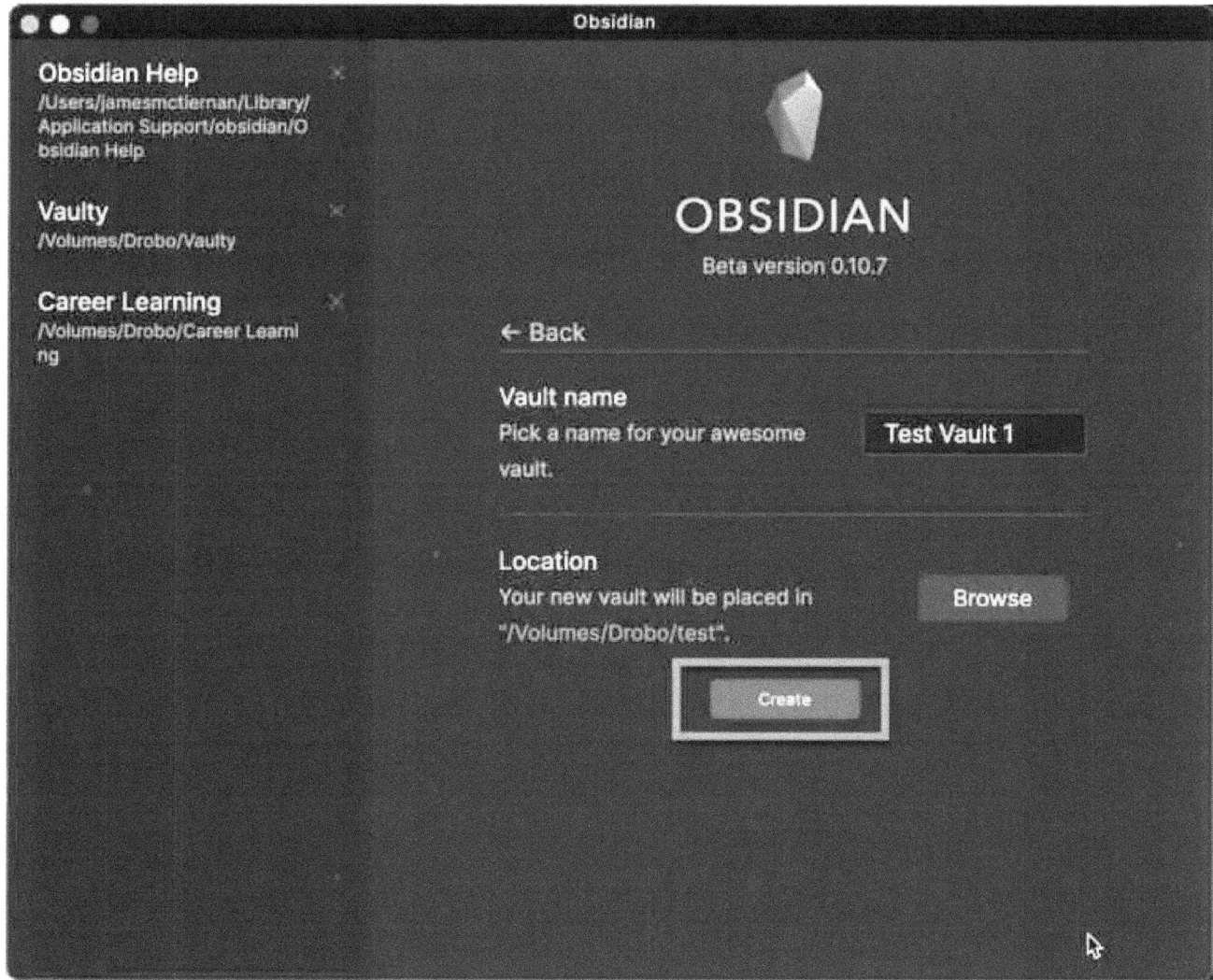

Once done, then you are good to go.

Next is to get acquainted with Obsidian's user interface and how to navigate around, what every pane and section is for, and the relevant shortcuts.

Interface

The screenshot below is how your Obsidian interface will look after installing and creating your master vault; with this, you are ready to start. The left section has details of the commands to navigate around Obsidian conveniently. You will see the files, folder panel, and section to create your first note.

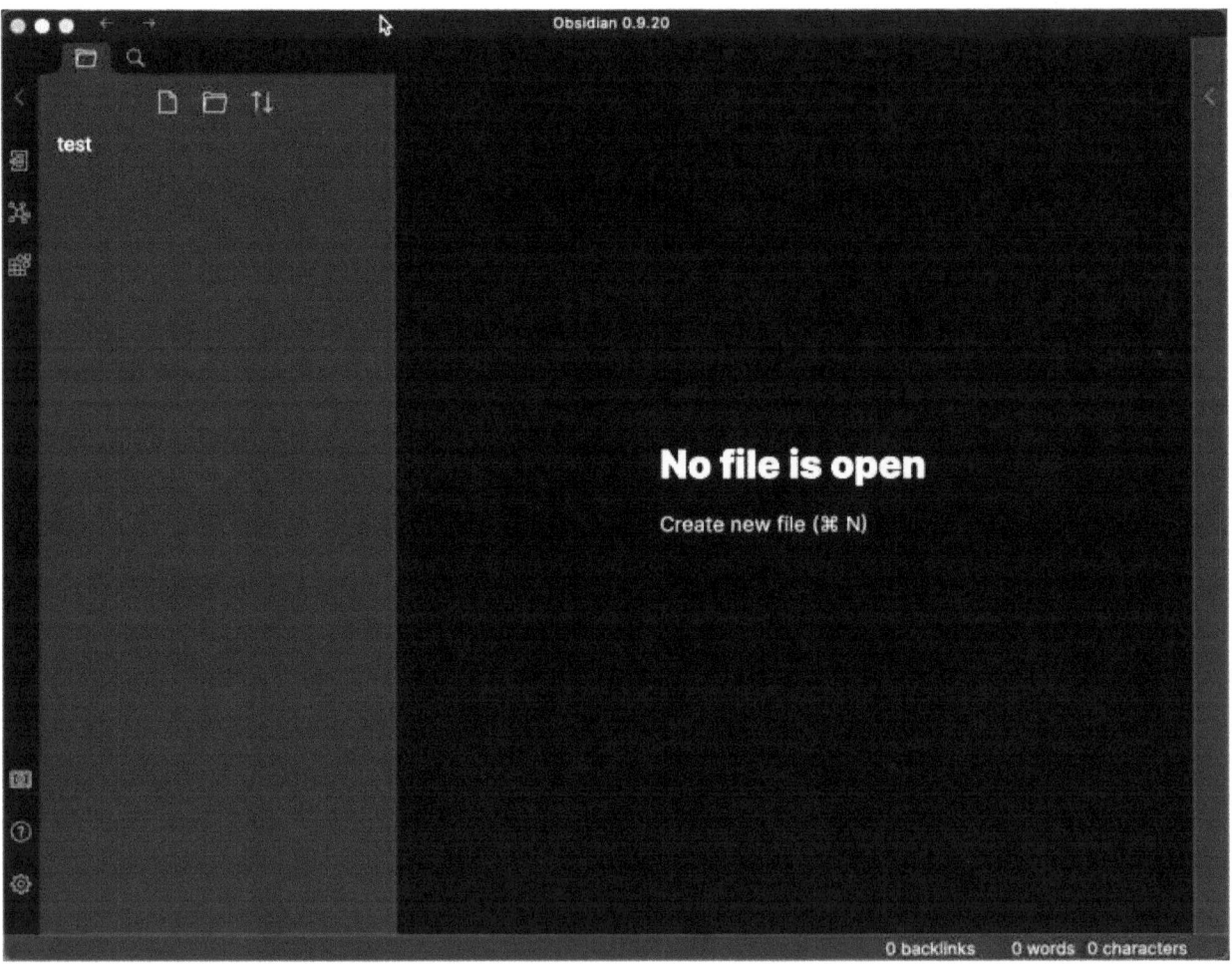

At its basic, the home screen is quite uncluttered and contains four sections. These sections contain the basic commands you will need to conveniently take notes and interact effectively with the interface. Other extra buttons around the toolbars are optional and will be discussed later in this guide. These sections include:

Toolbar

The essential tools are located at the far left and can be hovered over to learn more about them. This section also houses the "open graph view", which would be very useful when you have many notes. We will discuss this in detail very soon.

Files/Folders Section

This part of the application holds the relevant notes taken in the App. Additionally, you have buttons for making new files and folders. By activating some toggle buttons, you can move files into new folders with syntaxes or simply drag and drop. Also, you can collapse folders to access the content inside.

Active document

This is where you see active notes you are currently working on. However, you can create your first note in this blank space by pressing Ctrl or CMD +N for new files or Ctrl or CMD + O to access an already saved note.

Links Directory

You can see every link you created for the current document to the right of the interface. You can also make unlinked remarks (unlinked mention) on the current note if you don't want to forget an idea or comment.

Below is a screenshot of the different sections of the interface. Note, section 4 will only be seen when you click on the **"Expand"** button by the top right. You can also **"Collapse"** it with same button:

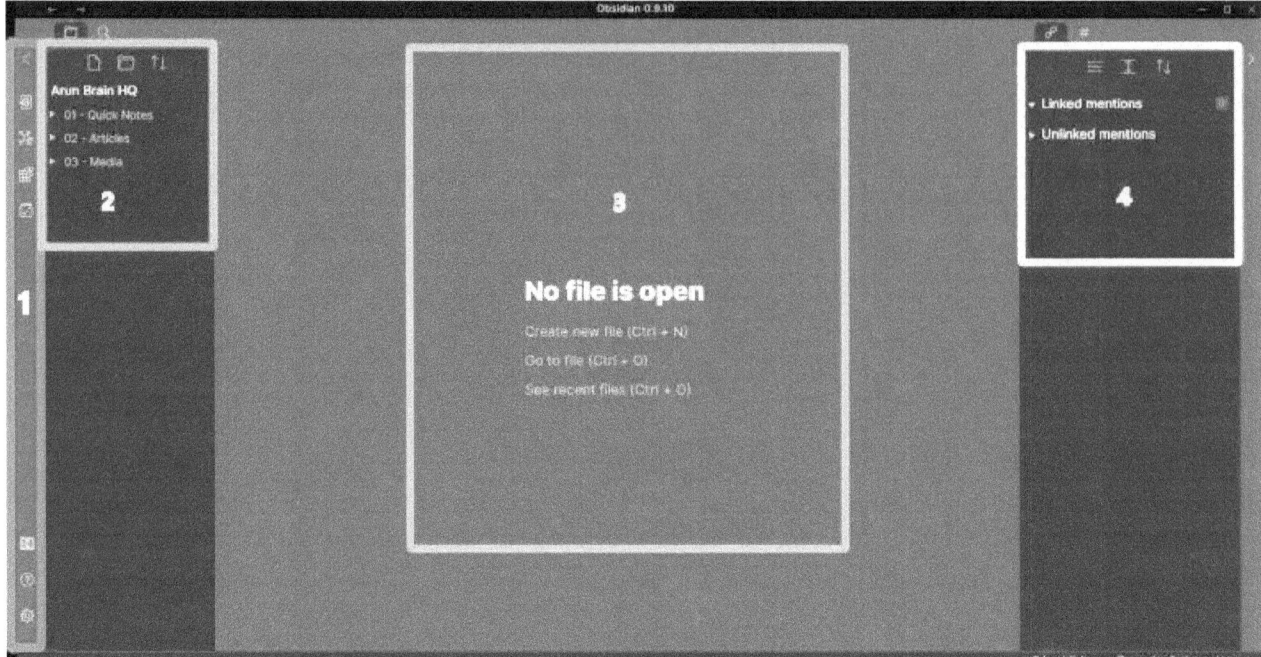

Left-Most Panel (Top Left)

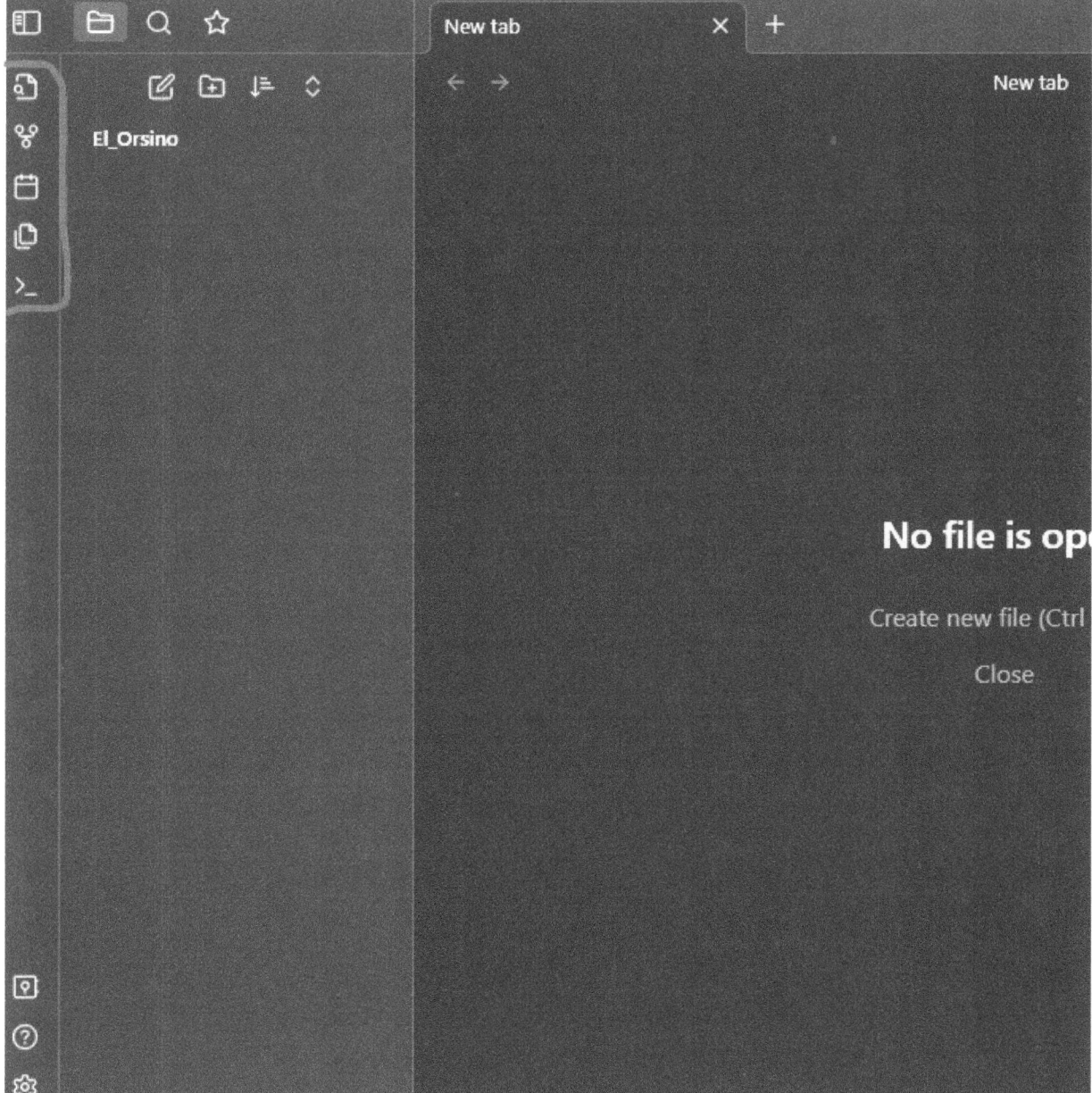

The extreme left pane contains four main icons, as shown in the screenshot above:

Open Quick Switcher

This section is used to quickly open pages by typing the name of the page in the text box, as shown in the screenshot below.

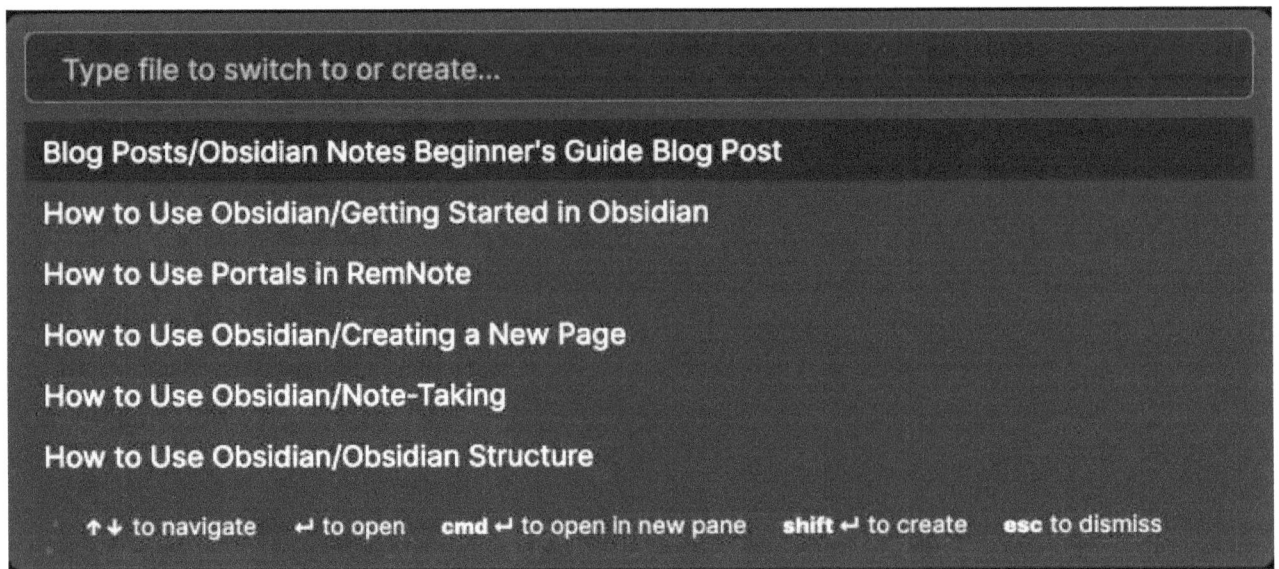

Open Graph View

This will display a graph showing the connections between each note/page. Later in this guide, we will go over this in detail.

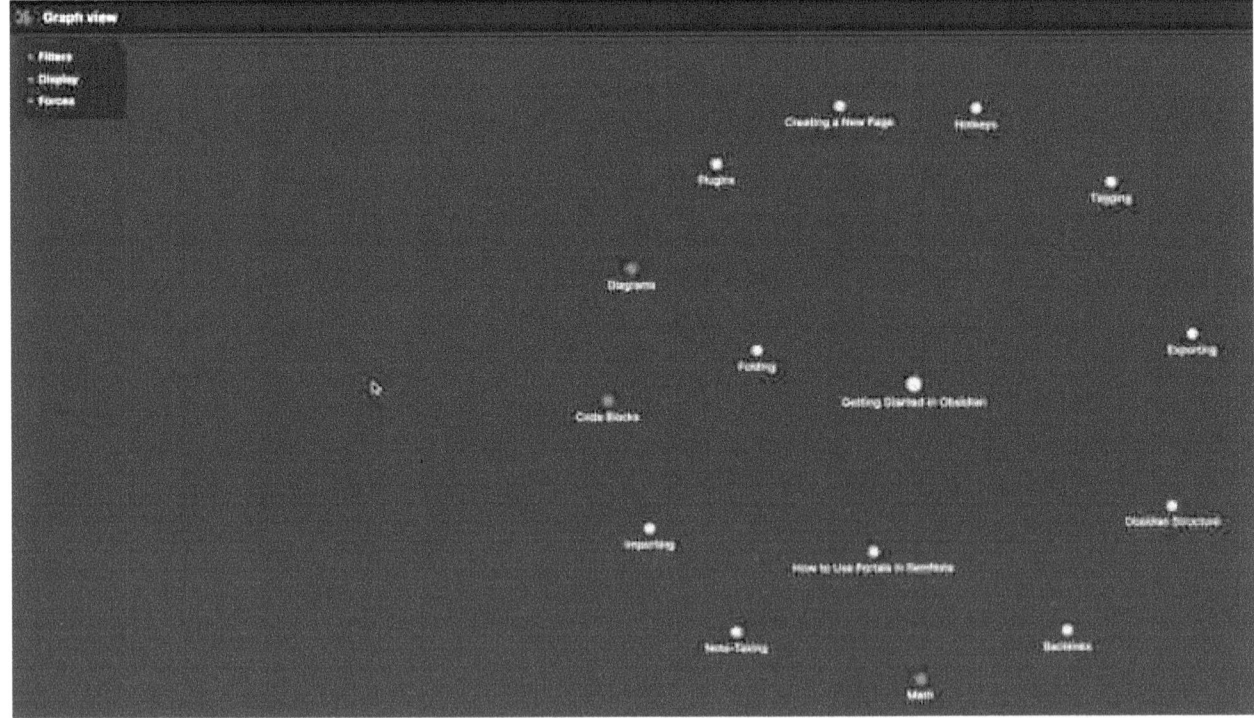

Open today's daily note

Once clicked, it automatically opens the section where you need to start inputting your note, with the exact date. See the screenshot below:

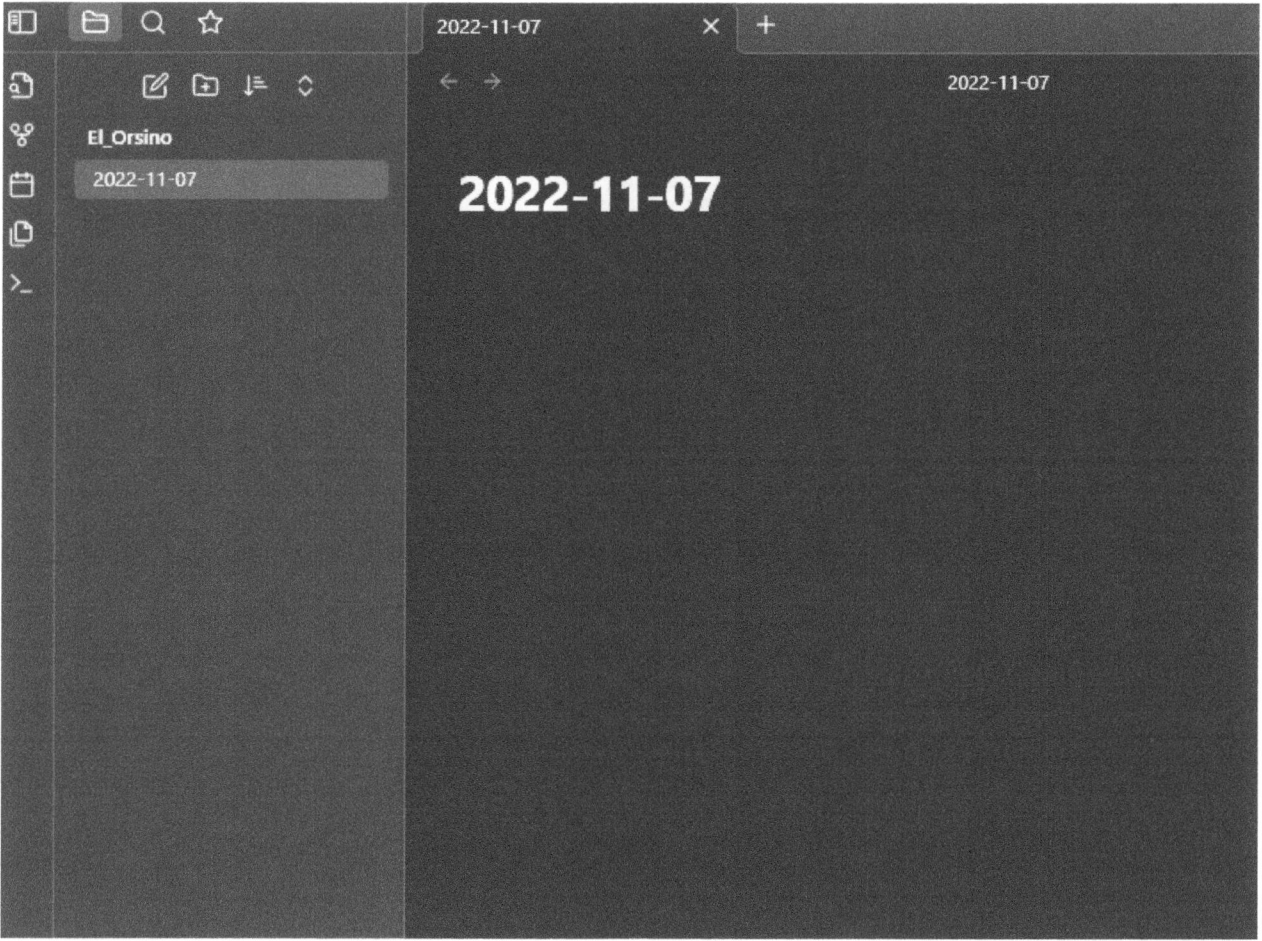

Collapse Panel

This is used to basically collapse the entire left-most pane. It opens the command palette once initiated.

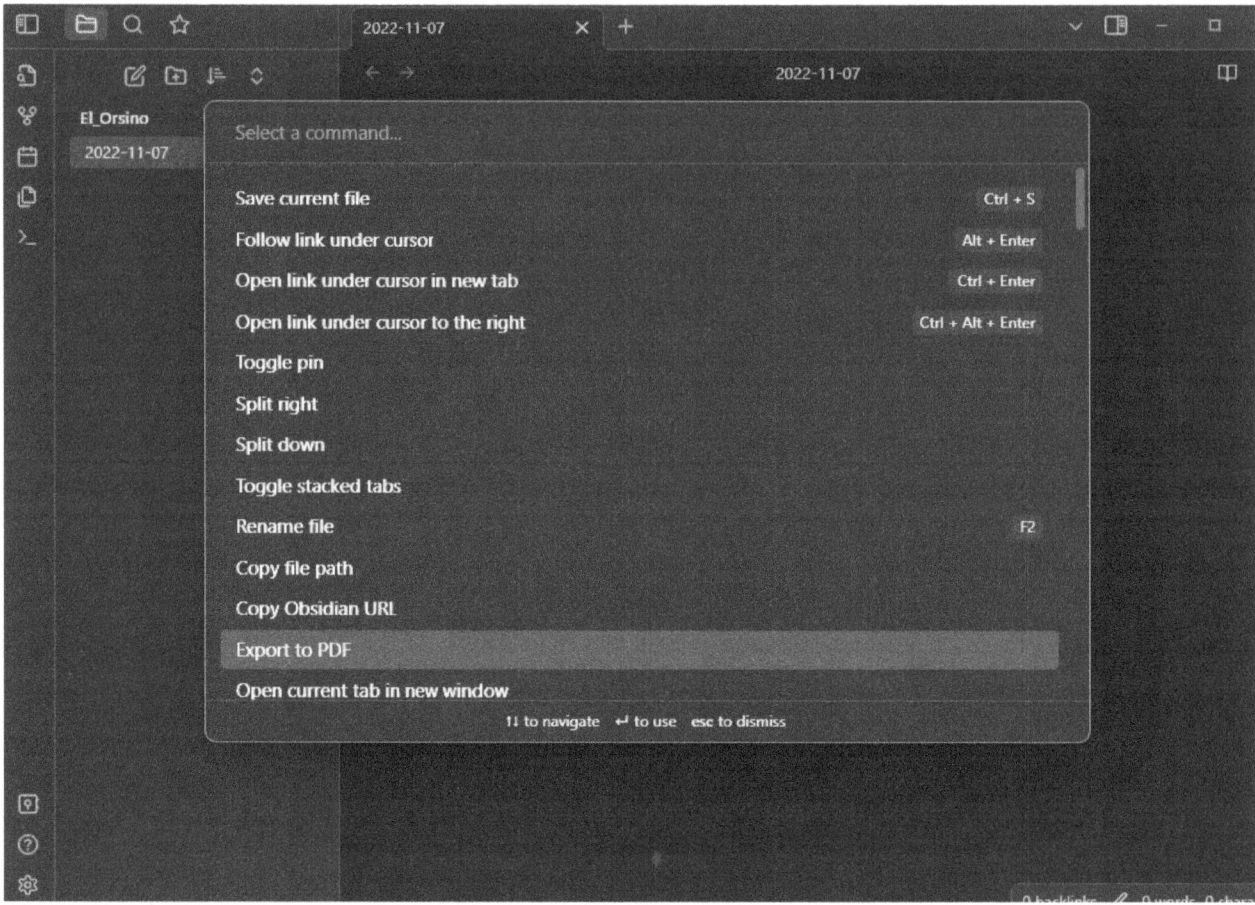

Left-Most Pane (bottom left)

There are three other buttons at the bottom left of the left-most pane; these include Open Another Vault, Help and Settings, respectively, as shown in the screenshot below:

Open Another Vault

By clicking on this button, you can access and open up another vault when a pop-up window is prompted, like the screenshot showing below; you can create a new vault or open already existing ones.

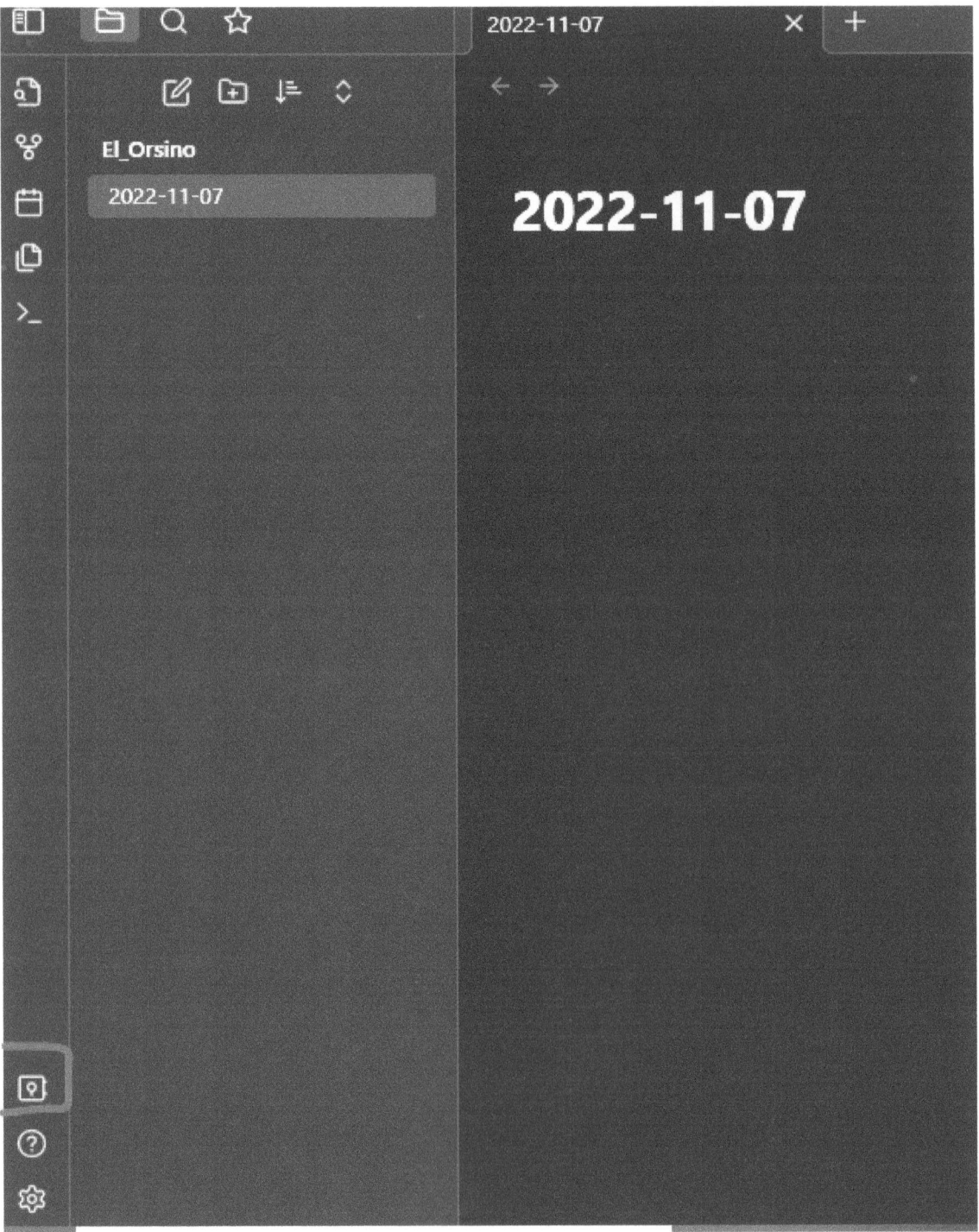

As you click on the "Open another vault" icon, it will initiate the next window to create a new vault.

Help

The screenshot below shows when you click on the help button, which is denoted by a question mark enclosed by a circle. This section helps you find your way around Obsidian, as the developers carefully document all the functionalities and features for easier use.

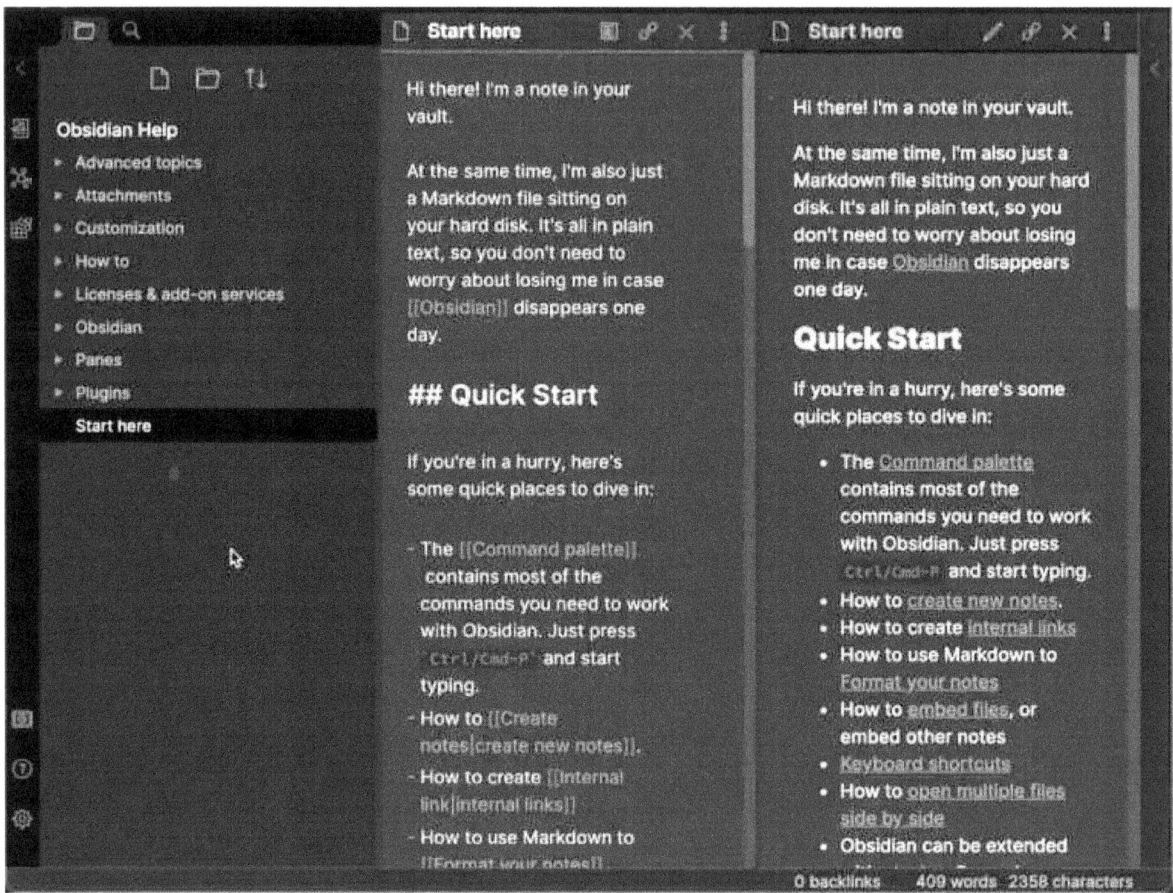

Settings

With the settings button, you can initiate a lot of settings like Setting Up Hotkeys, HTML to Markdown conversion while pasting a custom theme, initiating default and external plug-ins, changing appearance, and turning On and Off the spell check.

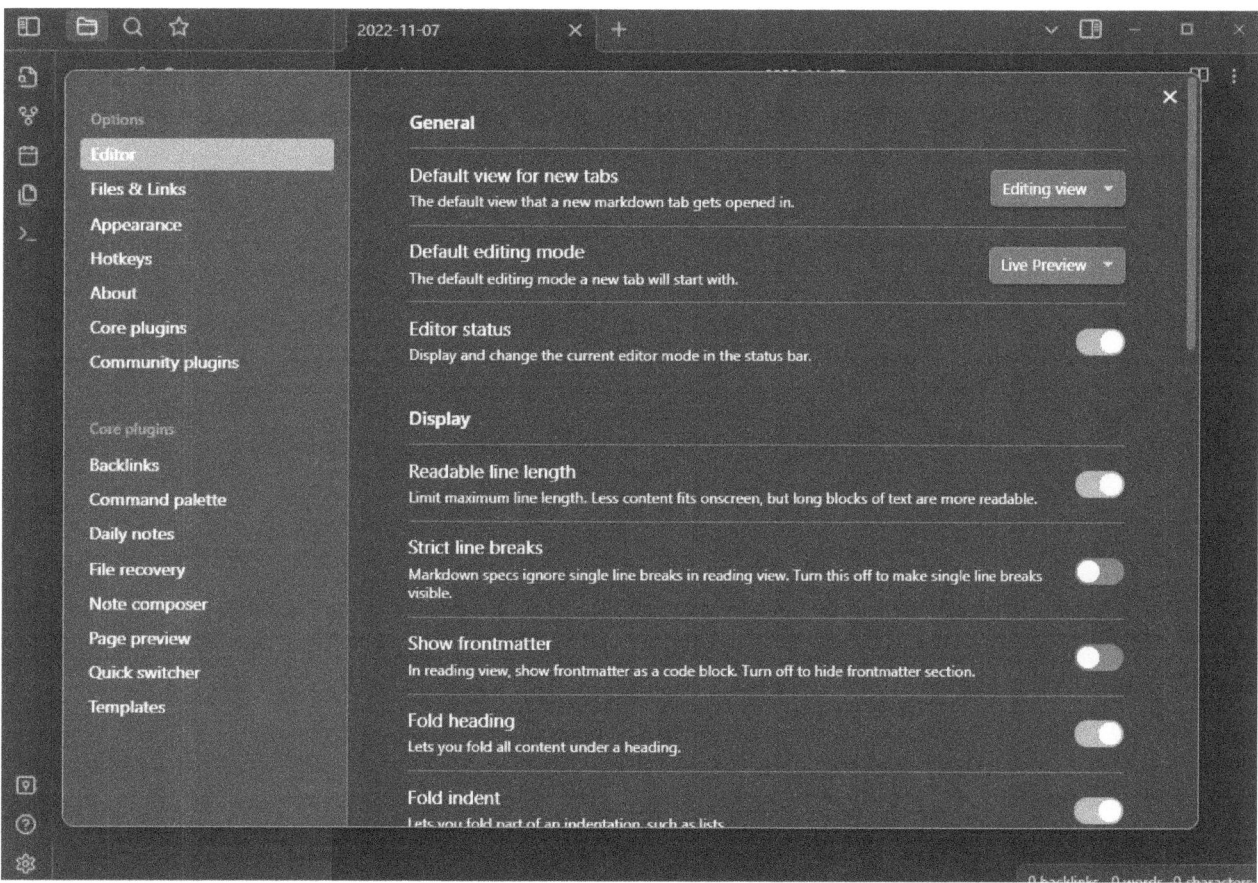

Basic Settings

There are a few optional buttons, while others are turned on by default. Since we will mainly deal with slid buttons in this section, it will be best to follow my lead as we synchronize the key features with the App. In the settings section, we mostly have subsections like the editor, plug-in, file & links, Appearance, Hotkeys, About Account, and Third-Party Plug-ins. However, below is a step-by-step guide on setting each button.

Editor

Screenshots of how the Editor sub-section should be configured:

Step 1

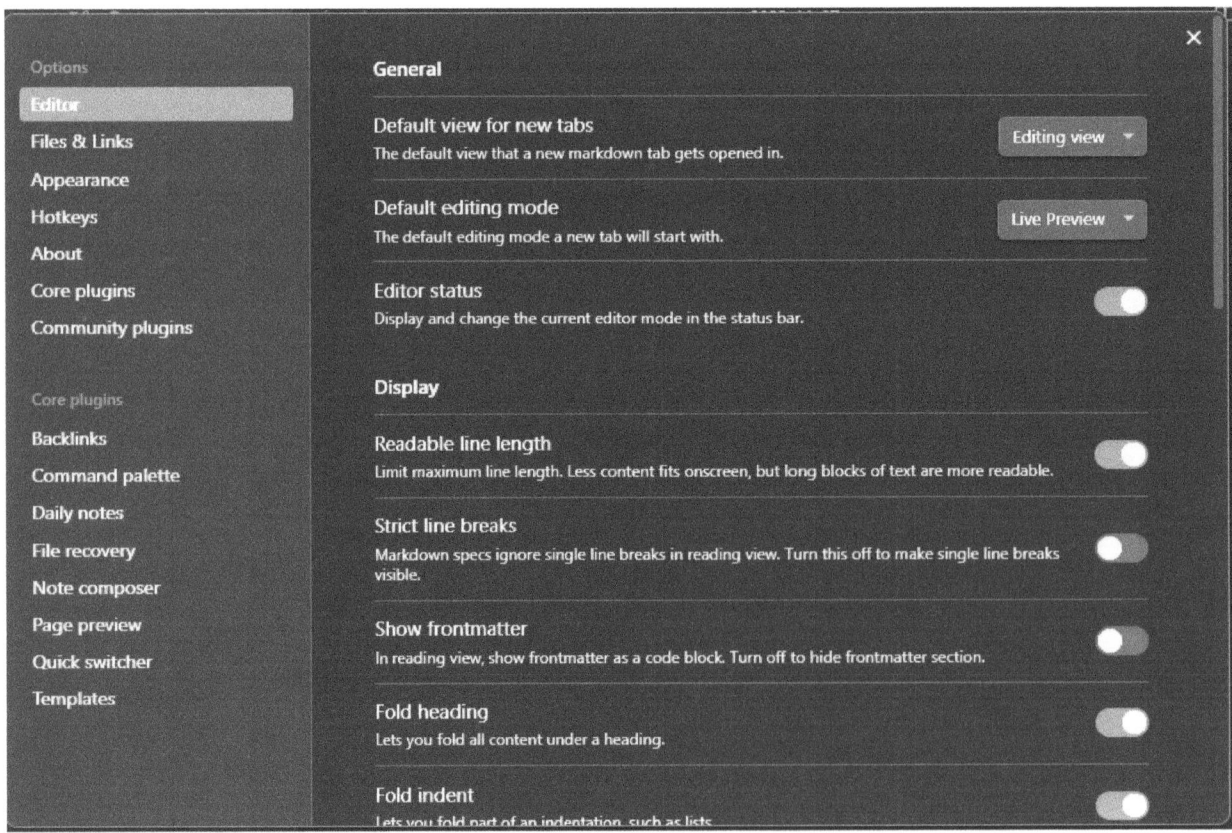

Step 2

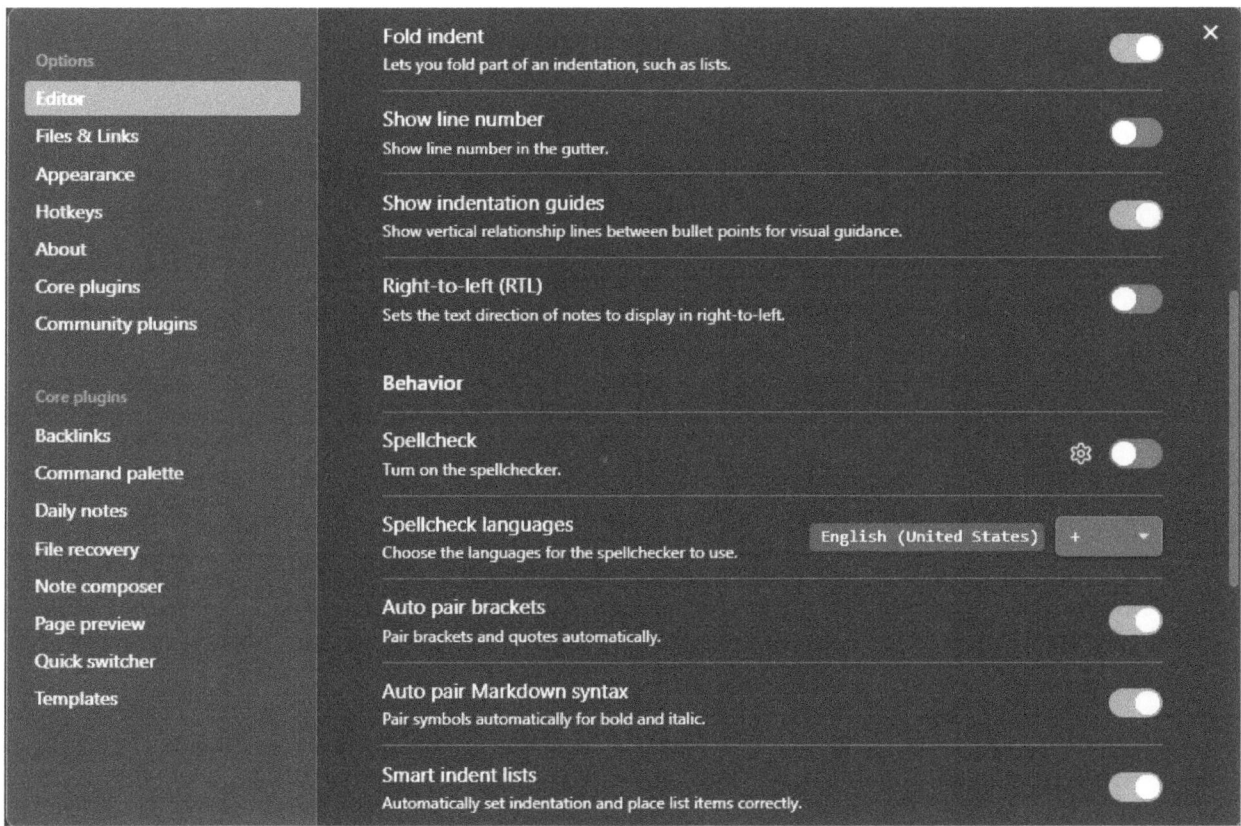

Step 3

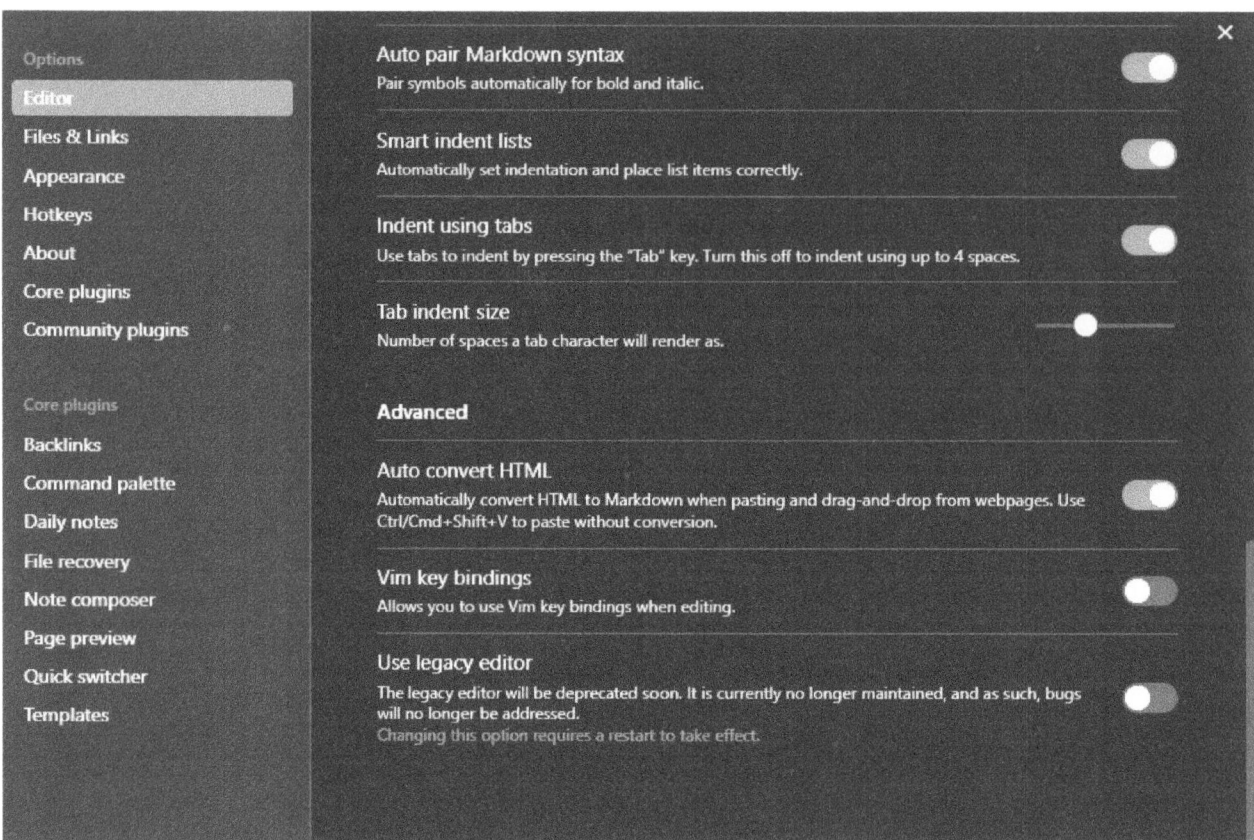

File & Links

How to configure the Files & Links sub-section:

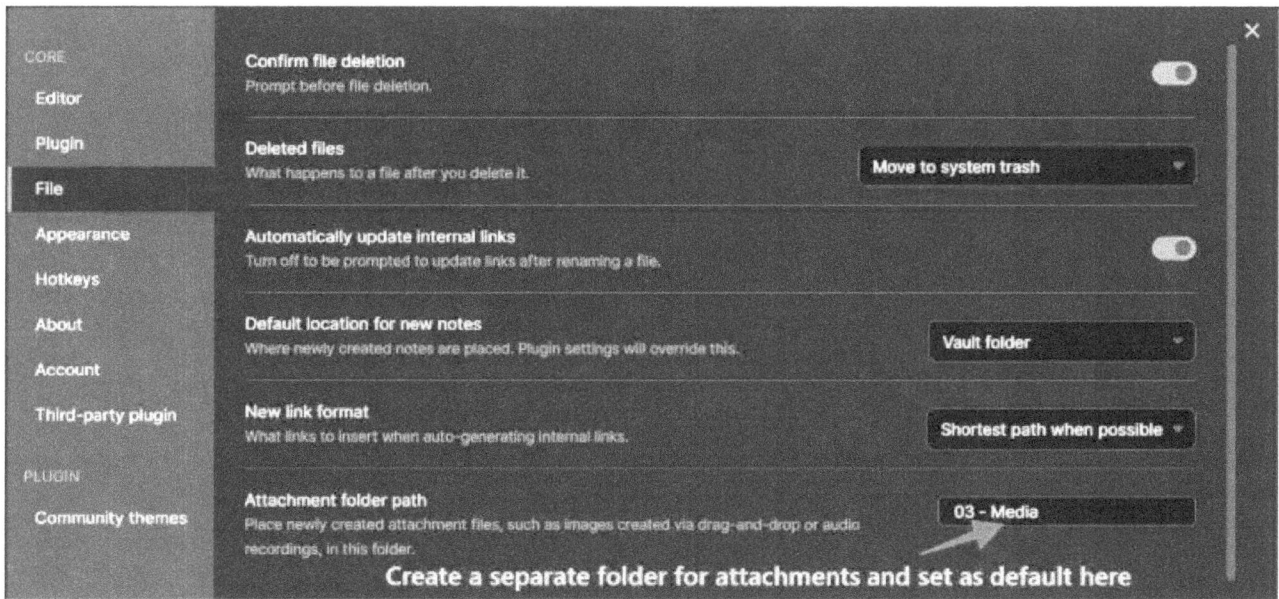

Appearance

How to configure the Appearance sub-section:

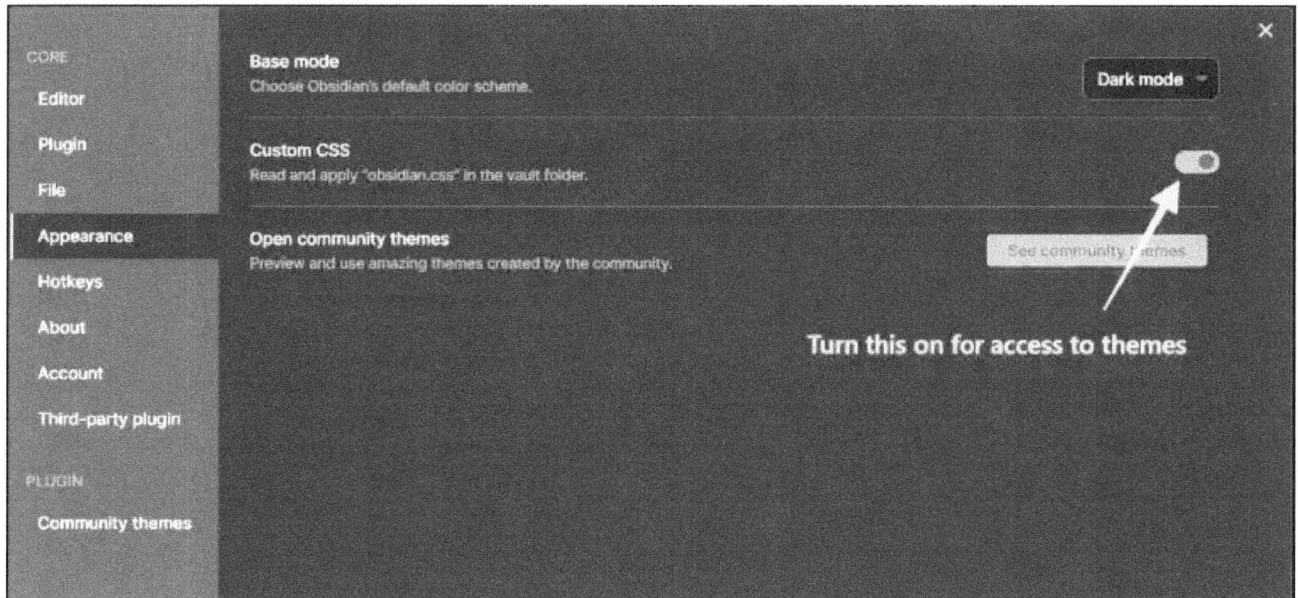

Note: For the other sub-sections, I suggest you leave them at their default settings. However, you can see updates on recent developments via the about sub-section. You can personalize the interface of your Obsidian App via the Community Themes section.

Hotkeys

Here is where you assign commands to keys to take specific action. We will get into details about it later in the guide:

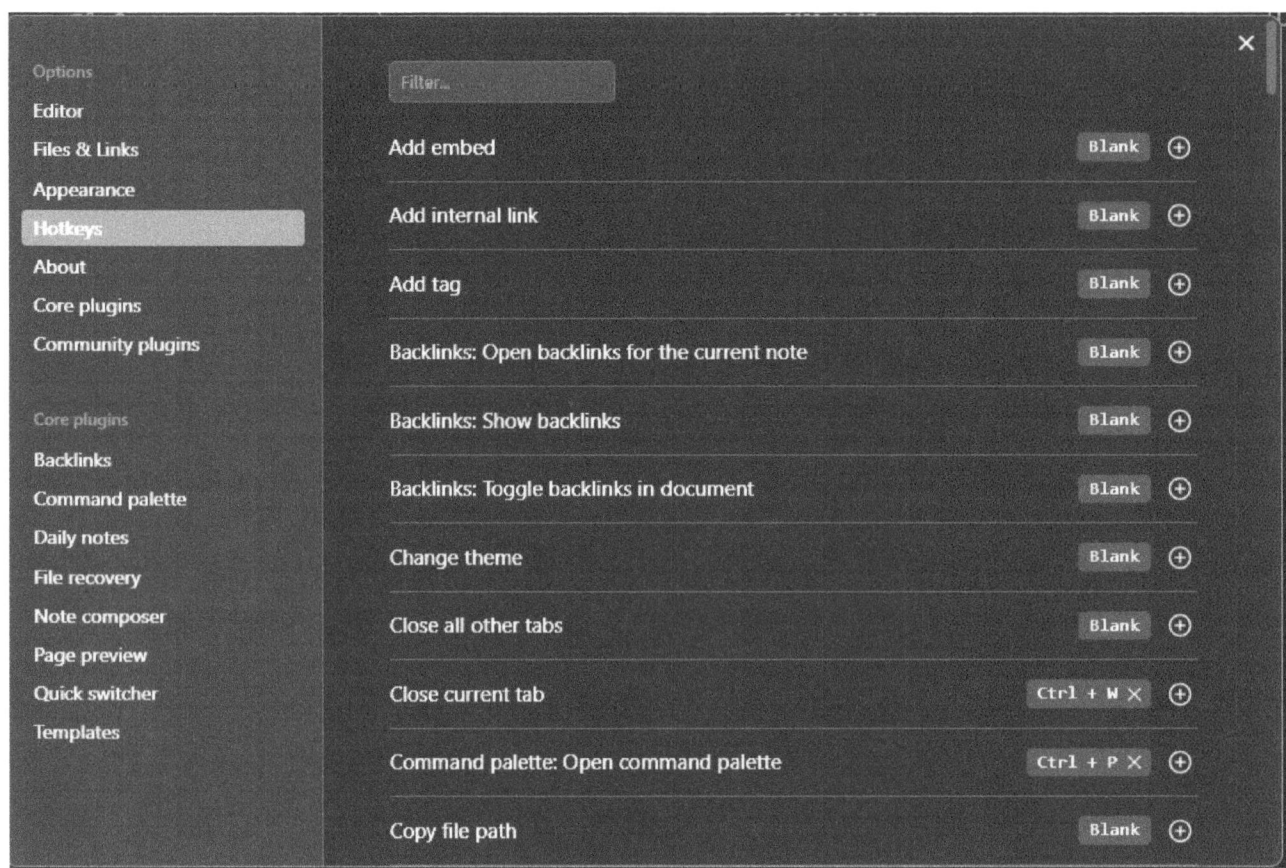

Core Plug-in

The practically limitless customization choices provided by Obsidian play a significant role in its current level of popularity. With the help of plug-ins, you can comfortably change how the interface looks and integrate other useful platforms into your Obsidian App.

Plug-ins are a vital part of your success with the App, but in the vein, it is important to select which you intend to use carefully. Understand the functionality and evaluate if you need it anyway, depending on your goal.

That said, core plug-ins are built-in plug-ins that launch as default options. To activate Core plug-ins.

Step 1: Go to the settings section

Step 2: Select Core Plug-in

Step 3: Choose your preferred plug-in by toggling the slide button off or on.

Screenshots of how the Core Plug-in sub-section should be configured:

Step 1

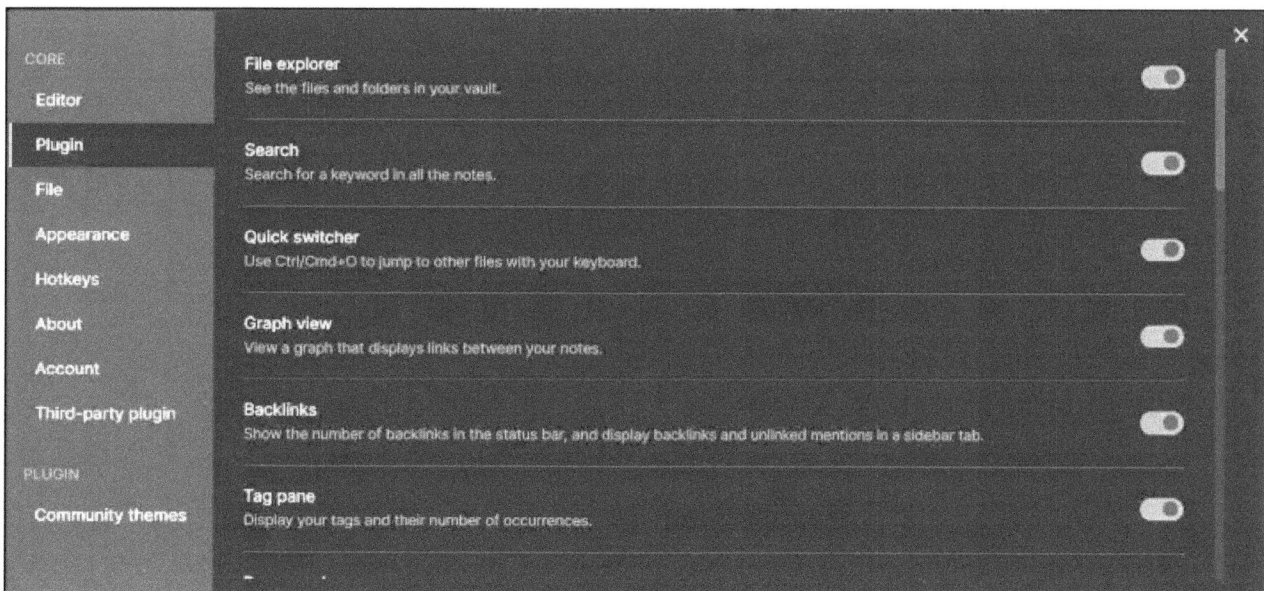

Step 2

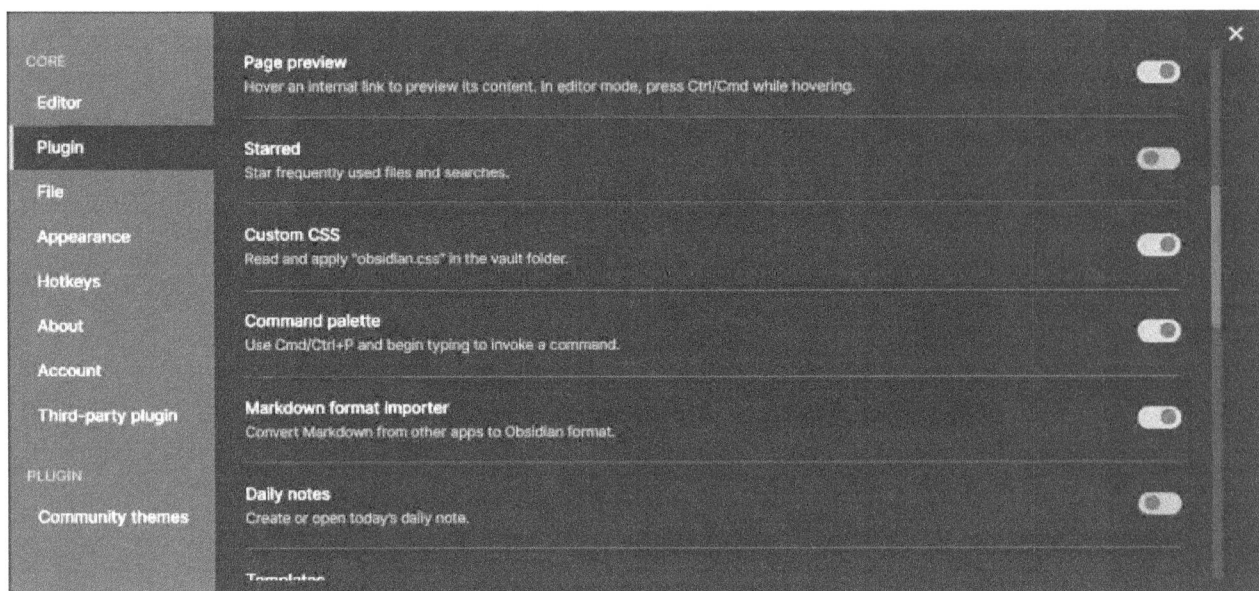

Step 3

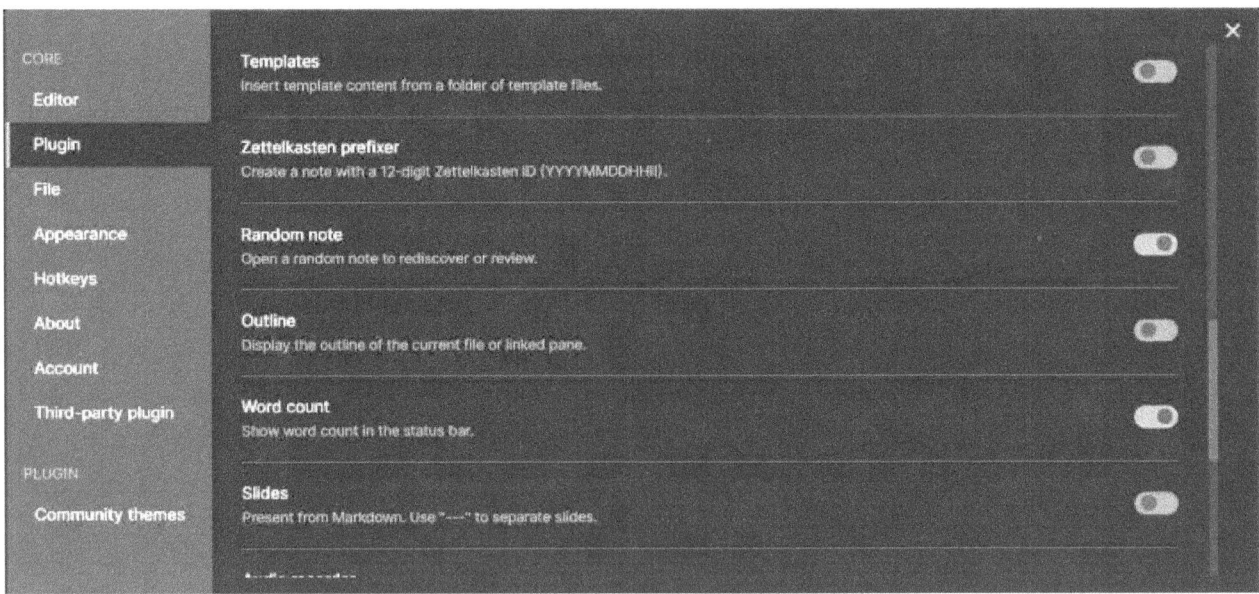

Step 4

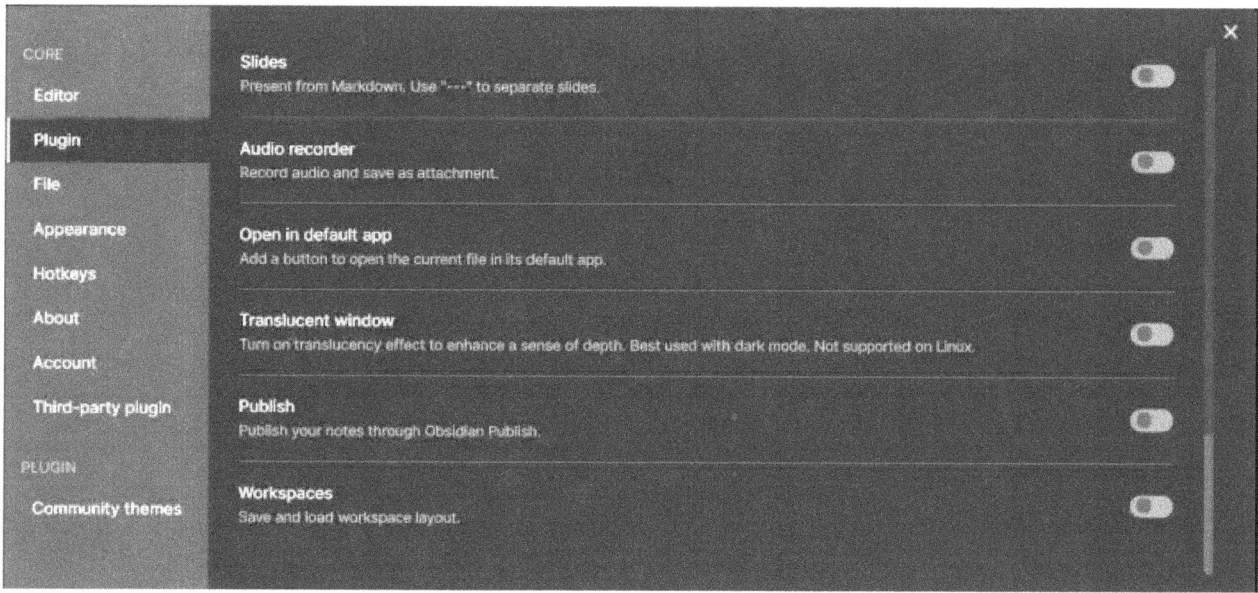

Important Core Plug-ins to use in your Obsidian

The core plug-ins are built into the program. Additionally, there are community-based plug-ins. And they are very handy in helping reduce the use of Notepads and stress with conventional note-taking systems.

Daily notes

Daily notes are an essential component of Obsidian, and they are also an essential component that will enhance your efficient use of Obsidian. Daily notes are notes you can link to a certain day. These notes have a unique naming system where the note's name is formed using the date. Because of this, it can be used to relate additional notes to this date. Obsidian is aware of every note's "backlinks" or all of the other notes in your Vault connected to it. The best part is you can automate your notes, and we will address that later in this guide.

Daily notes in Obsidian can also serve as a sort of index to many of your other notes. This will generally replace your imagined timeline in a Notepad.

You can activate daily notes under Settings > Core Plug-ins.

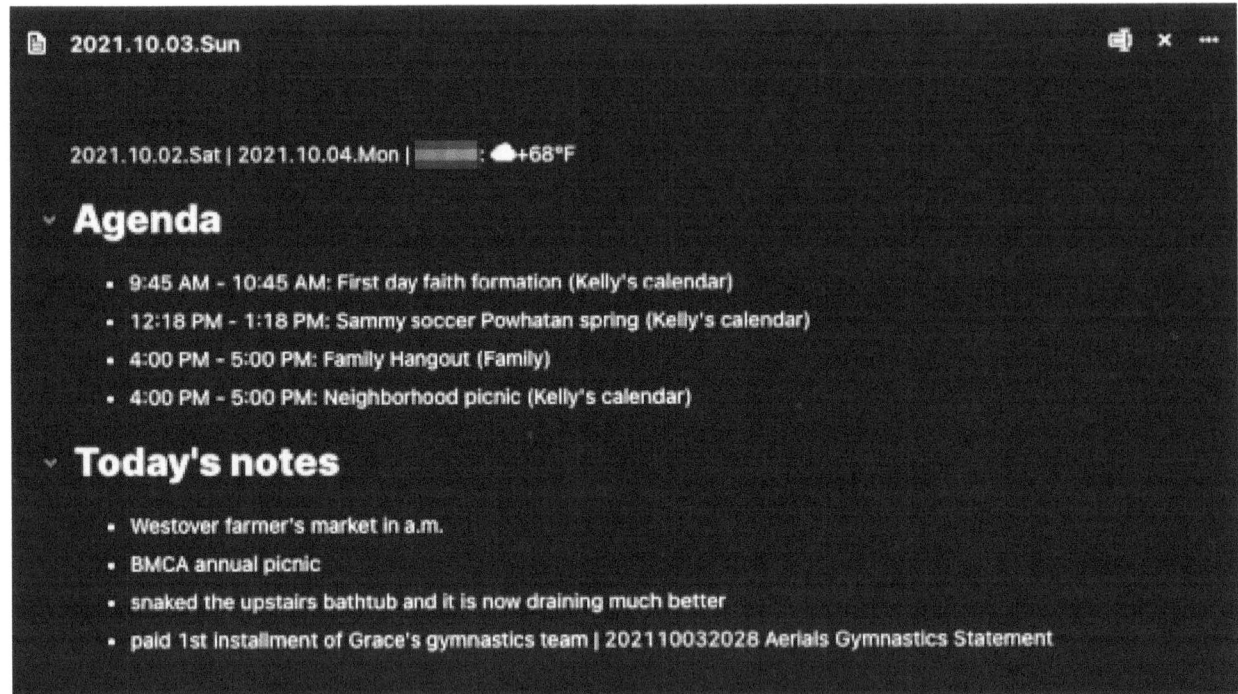

Starred notes

This is sure your best option if you don't like wasting time. It helps you access more notes quickly, especially notes you regularly use at any given time. This is the purpose of "starred" notes. You can "**star**" a note after enabling this core plug-in from the Settings > Core Plug-ins

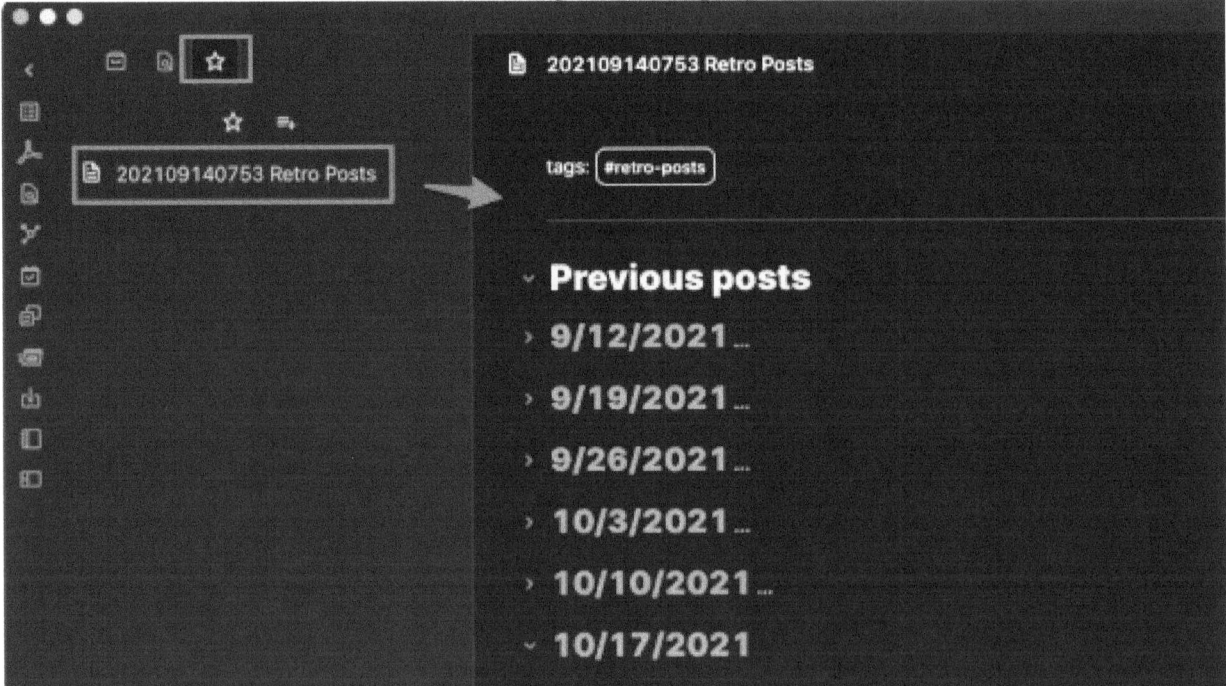

menu. When a note is starred, it becomes immediately accessible from the Star panel on the left side of the screen.

Zettelkasten prefixer

This one has a long name but describes an intriguing system for keeping notes organized. You might not need to use it for all your notes, but you can use it while creating your note (especially a reading note). Obsidian has developed into a helpful tool for those who want to have a digital Zettelkasten format because of its ability to link notes and clearly show their relationships.

Anyway, let's get back to the reason for discussing this plug-in. With the Zettelkasten prefixer, you can do two things:

1. It enables you to choose a "prefix" based on a date format for your note titles. You can use number combinations like 202110111506. This is not a complex analysis; it is just a combination of the date and time of creating the note using the yyyymmddhhmm format. Obsidian automatically adds the prefix when you use one to create a note, and you can choose to add more to the title. It may not seem like much, but having the date in this format has much power. With this illustration, you can easily search by date when looking for notes.
2. You can, at your discretion, set a template for your note so that, when it is created, it has additional data in addition to the title prefix. This can speed up the process and promote standardization.

When you add a new note, the screenshot below shows how your default template will show:

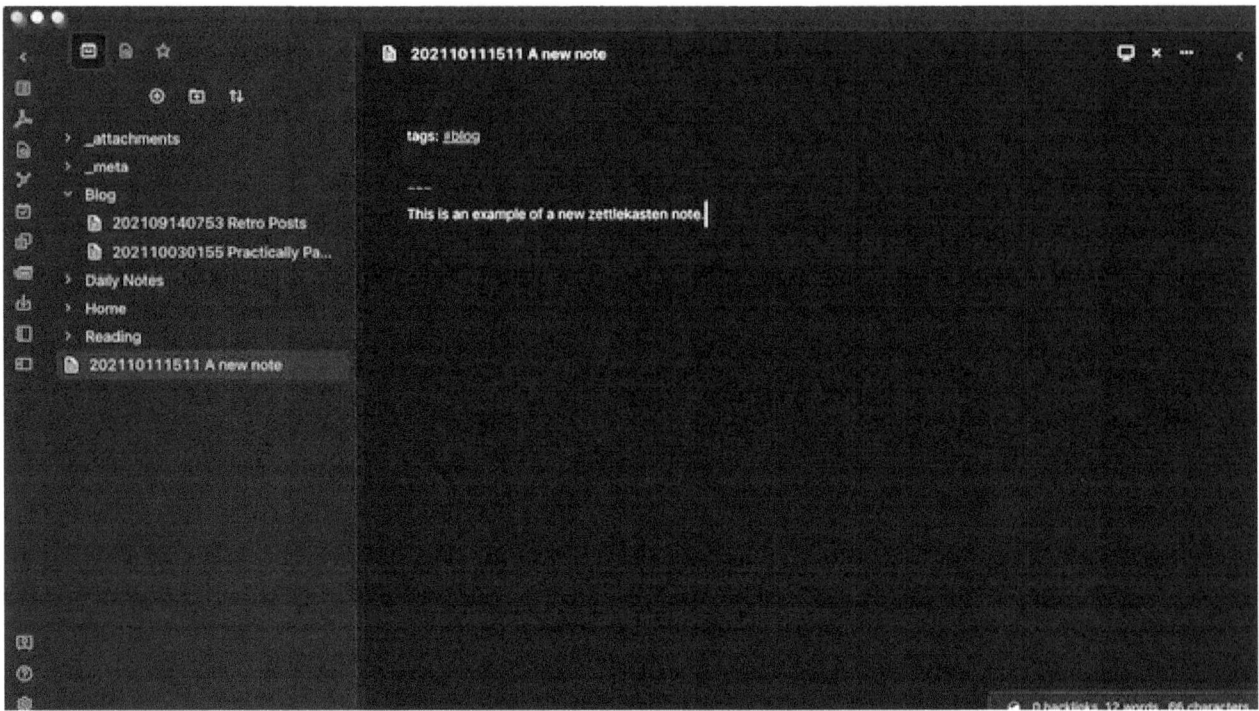

How to Name Notes with Zettelkasten prefixer core plug-in in Obsidian

The prefix is used to give a note title its own identity. The screenshot below shows a screen where the plug-in is being activated. You simply have to search for it, then toggle the slide button to turn it on or off.

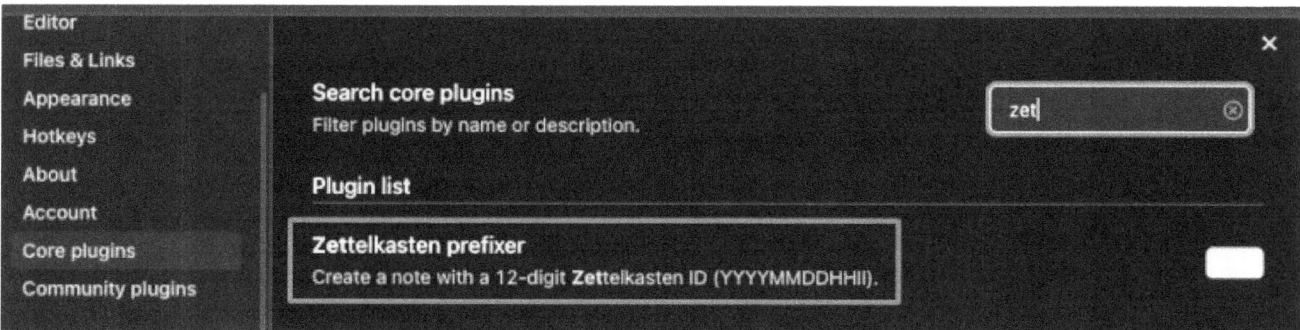

Obsidian already has this plug-in; it does not need to be added independently via the community plug-ins. So will then have to set up the Zettelkasten prefix as illustrated below:

You will need to assign a shortcut to this process, as illustrated in the shortcut section on creating a new one. We used Opt + Z on Mac to initiate the process for this demonstration. So let's explain what each of these sections will do:

- New file location: This is where you initially save any new notes made. However, since our demonstration is empty, we can enter the Vault at the highest level. After you create them, you manually move them by dragging and dropping them.
- Template file location: You can make each for every note to make sure there are unique. You will see those templates in this section. Templates are simply markdown files with

all the same capabilities as markdown files. You can make a simple one with templates to add tags.

- Zettel ID format: This is how the number is presented. You can still use the YYYMMDDHHmm format.

To make this simpler to use, you can try some simple changes. It will help if you activate a shortcut for initiating a new Zettelkasten note. The "Create new Zettelkasten not" function is bound to the hotkey as stated below:

As I suggested earlier, use Opt + Z; by pressing that, you will get an interface in the screenshot below:

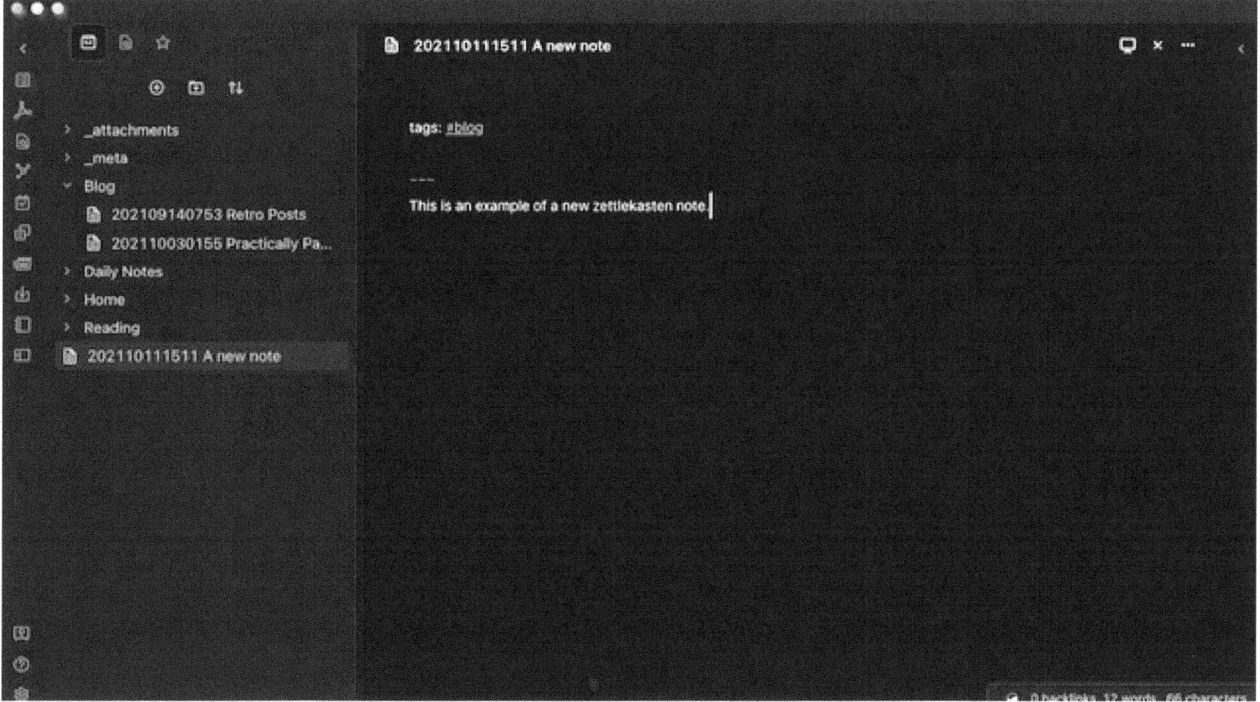

Like many others, using a Zettelksaten prefix on notes is advantageous for some vital reason. For example, you can quickly make notes using a template without worrying about giving it a full title. This is helpful for fast notes that I want to make without taking too much time to consider a title. And can always return to them in the future.

Not so many know about this, but below is an approach to help sort notes by dates in the title because the Zettelkasten prefix depends on the current date and time. Let's say we want to use all the files we made around October 2021. We can easily file them by typing **file: 202110** and seeing all the notes created within that date, as shown below in the screenshot.

```
file: 202110                                    ⊗

202110 011015 Fexibo Sit-Stand Desk
202110 030155 Practically Paperless
202110 031950 Articles I've read
202110 032000 Collections and permanance
202110 032004 Unpacking My Library
202110 032028 Aerials Gymnastics Statement
202110 041419 Specializing versus expanding
202110 060841 Knucleballs
202110 060842 The Baseball 100
202110 201500 Cicada Queen by Bruce Sterli...
202110 202140 Beyond the Dead Reef by Ja...
202110 211609 Year's Best Science Fiction V...
202110 211611 Slow Birds by Ian Watson
202110 211616 Vulcan's Forge by Poul Ande...
202110 212007 Ideas
202110 221104 Man-Mountain Gentian by H...
202110 221338 Hardfought by Greg Bear
202110 231108 Manifest Destiny by Joe Hald...
202110 231111 Full Chicken Richness by Avr...
202110 251131 GitHub
202110 251144 Covid Vaccination Card - Ja...
202110 251145 Covid Vaccination Card - Zach
202110 251716 E. B. White on hoarding
202110 251717 E. B. White on Sputnik
202110 251719 E. B. White on Writing
Pasted image 202110 18154733.png
```

For Community /Third Party Plug-in

Obsidian gives room for developers outside the platforms team to create plug-ins that are compatible with the system. These plug-ins are categorized under the Community plug-in. However, it might not be as safe as the core plug-ins, and you will need to grant access.

To activate, select "Turn on community plug-in" at the bottom of the pop-up window after going to Settings, then Community plug-ins to access community plug-ins.

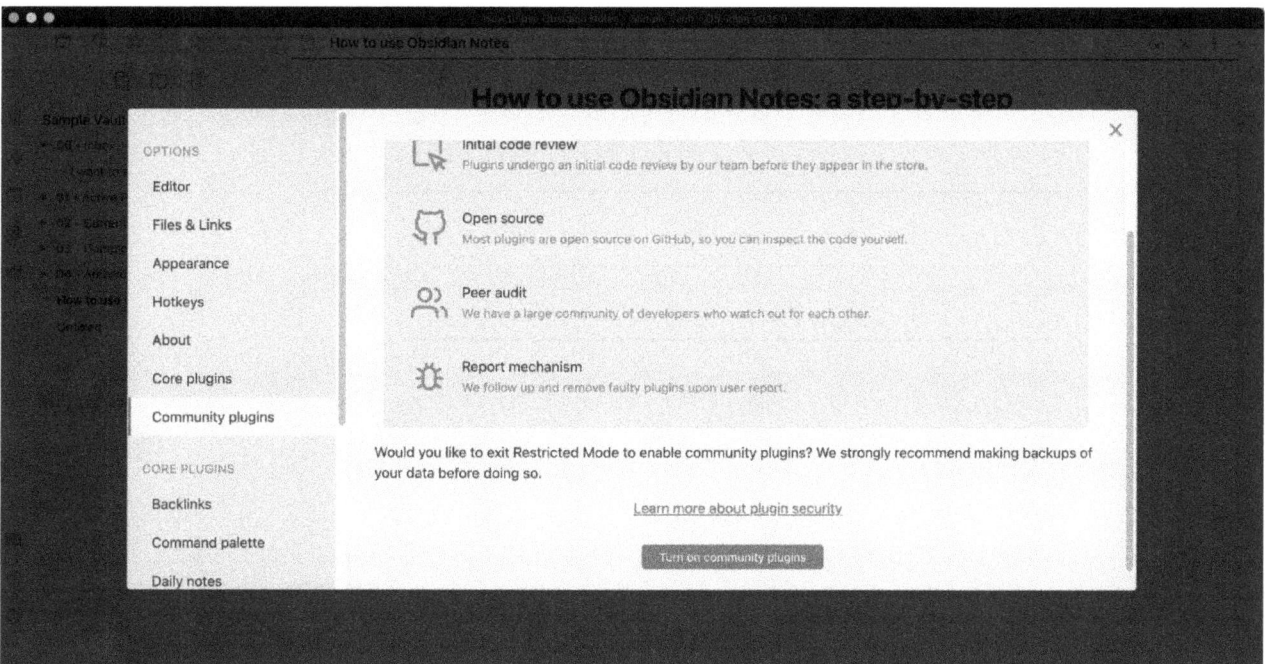

After granting access through the opt-in window, you will be allowed to search through and choose from many plug-ins. Below is a list of some commonly used community plug-ins:

- Advanced Tables Obsidian: A plug-in that helps with formatting and manipulating tables.
- Obsidian Underline: Plug-in that helps activate the ctrl or CMD + U shortcut that aids underlining texts and inserts the HTML markup.
- Obsidian Calendar Widget: Adds calendar to your Obsidian App
- Obsidian Outliner: Helps manage lists as in RoamResearch
- Zotero-Obsidian Integration: This plug-in allows users to import and insert bibliographies, notes, citations and PDF annotations into their Obsidian App from Zotero
- Raindrop-Obsidian Plug-in: Raindrop.io is a bookmarking platform, and this plug-in helps integrate the platform with Obsidian.

Shortcuts / Basic Formatting

Now that you know the basic information, it will be nice to show you some of the shortcuts you might need in the long run while using Obsidian.

Convert to Reading Mode

Obsidian is automatically on Live Preview Mode. Switch to "Editing Mode" by pressing Ctrl or CMD + P to show the command palette the choose 'Reading Mode."

Command Palette

Ctrl P will bring up the interface below:

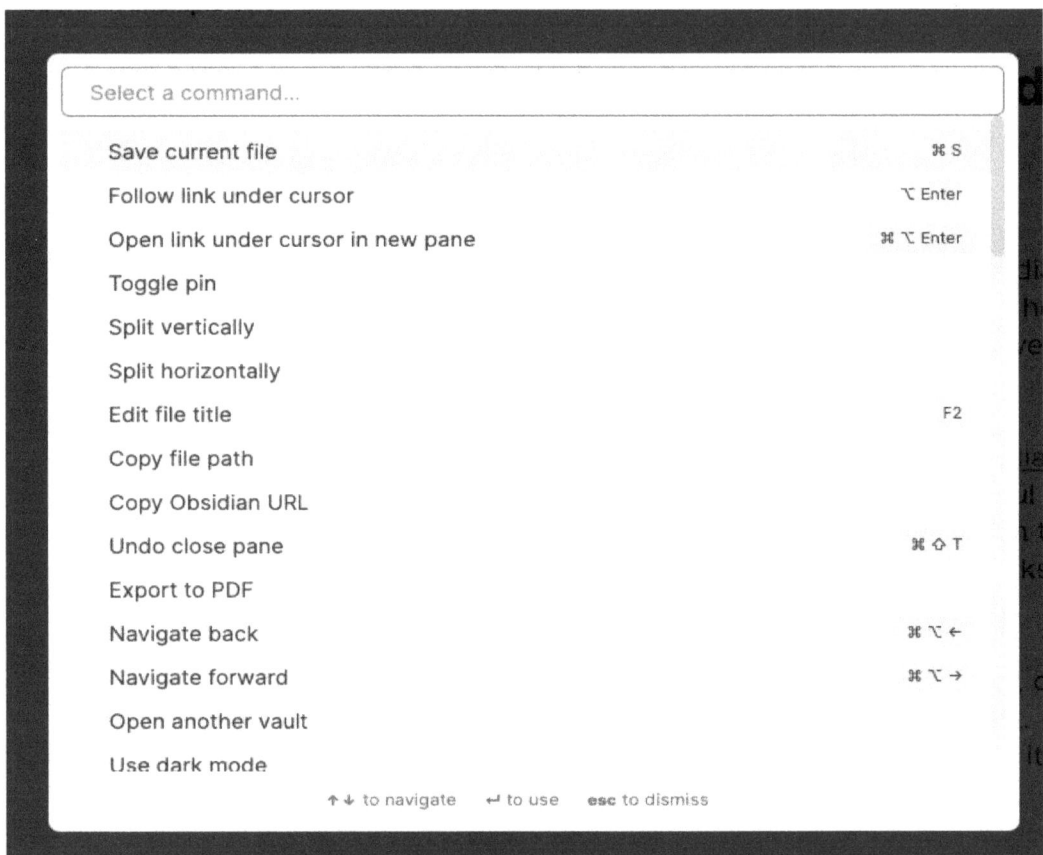

Create New Note

To make new notes, press Ctrl or CMD + N.

Close Window

To close that note window, use Ctrl or CMD + W.

Switch Between Notes

Hold Ctrl or CMD + Alt or OPT + Left/Right direction to move between the previous and next note.

Creating New Internal Links

By pressing the square bracket **"[[" twice**, you can create a new internal link

Obsidian previews an internal link's content once the cursor hovers over it.

Numbered or Bullet Point while making a list

Press 1. or – then space to start numbered or bullet list

For headings

Press #, then space for heading 1, or 2 ## for heading 2, and follow the same pattern for other headings.

Changing font in Obsidian

Follow these steps to change to your desired font in Obsidian App:

Step 1: Select the "Setting" cog

Step 2: Toggle the "Appearance" section

Step 3: Look under "Font" in the menu. The interface font, the text font, and other fonts can all be changed from here.

Note: It is possible to adjust the font size from here.

Adding Footnotes

If you want to add to your comments without altering your workflow, footnotes are your best chance of doing so. Since there are not also built-in, you will need to install the "Footnote Shortcut" plug-in.

It will be a markup .txt, looking like this:

Text with footnote: [^1]

Hello World

[^1]: Footnote

For easy activation, add ^[Foot Note Text] to the end of the text.

Additionally, footnotes can be added straight into the text by doing so:

This text is a sample. The following text

A footnote is included in this paragraph.

(Footnote Text)

Creating Table on Obsidian

You can insert tables into text using the "Advance Table" plug-in from the community plug-in section. This makes it a lot easier to format and edit text that should be in a table.

After installing, you will need to input the following procedures to get a table:

| Syntax | Description |

| --------- | ----------- |

| Book | Pen |

| Ruler | Marker |

This will generate a table like the one below:

Heading	Description
Book	Pen
Ruler	Marker

To Bold Texts

Write your text between two star signs "**" to bold, or Ctrl or CMD + B.

Quotation

To start a quote, press > then space. \- and space followed by the quoter's name

Horizontal Line Split

To initiate a horizontal line split, press minus three times or use dashes with no space "---"and then enter.

However, if you place three dashes exactly under a text in an Obsidian note interface, it will convert to Heading 1.

Hyperlink

But for hyperlink link insertion, type Ctrl or CMD + K, enter the text in the square bracket, and the hyperlink in the usual brackets.

Graph View

To initiate the graph view on the note interface, press Ctrl or CMD + G

Opens Quick Switcher (File Browser)

Pressing Ctrl or CMD + O will initiate a quick file browse.

Edit Mode/ View Mode Toggle

To initiate the edit mode, press Ctrl or CMD + E

Strikethrough text

To strikethrough text, you need to enclose the sentence with "~~" For instance, "~~I love eating rice~~.

Highlighting Text

To highlight a text, you must enclose the sentence with a double "equal to" sign. For instance, "==I love eating rice==.

Underlining Text

Since Underline isn't built in as default in the App, you will need to install it via the community plug-in section, as explained in the plug-in section above. After installation, use Ctrl or CMD + U to initiate an underline. It might not look professional in Markdown, but it sure is the best option at this point.

Code blocks

Code blocks are helpful for two reasons. First, they prevent your editor from compiling the code. Secondly, the code will typically be properly highlighted for syntax.

Use the' (then type the programming language) followed by some codes to insert code. Like

"`HTML

Add the code here` "

Adding checklist

To add a checklist on Obsidian, use – [ ]

For instance,

- [ ] Name

- [ ] Address

Choosing a Theme

With all the information you have gotten to this extent, you are on the right part to creating your first note. So after installation and creating a Vault, the next thing will be to choose the best theme for your Obsidian interface. First, you will need to decide if you want your App in light or dark mode. To choose which theme you want,

Step 1: Go to the **Settings** section as shown above

Step 2: Click on the **Appearance** sub-section

Step 3: Use the dropdown menu to choose between the Light and Dark theme.

To customize the present theme further, use the back button to go back to the settings section. Then click on the **Community Themes** sub-section.

Next, click on **Use** to apply your preferred theme. Note: some themes can only be used for specific theme modes.

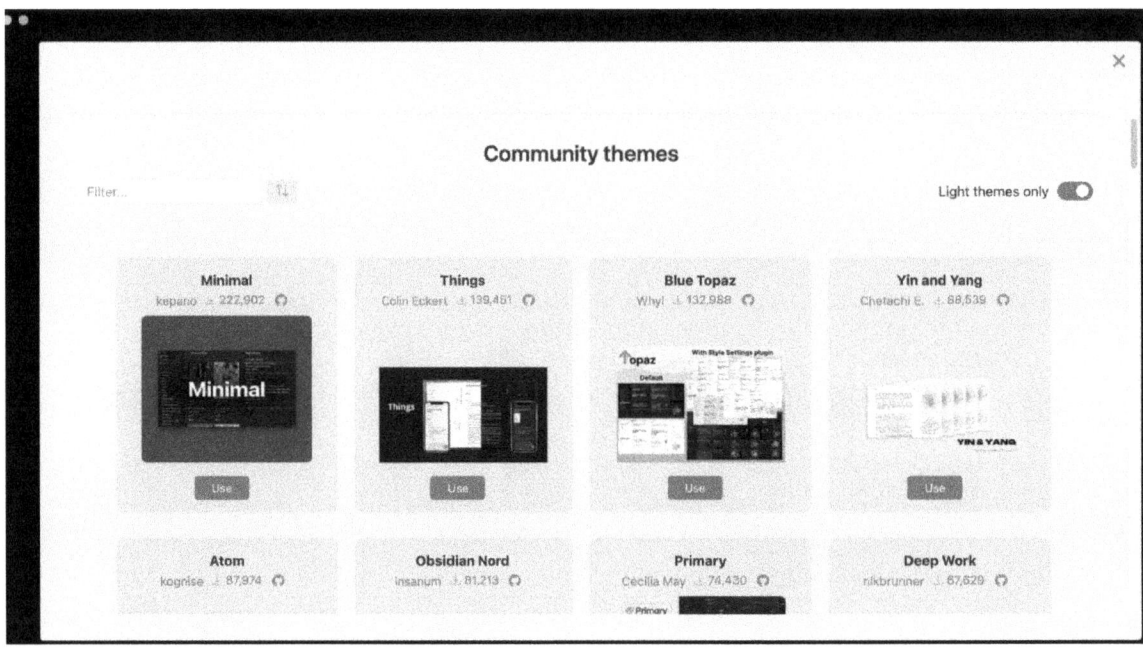

Setting Up Your Folders

After creating the Vault, the next will be creating folders (which are not obligatory). Instead of creating file structures to hold your notes, you can use links and backlinks if you think there are best. However, to create a folder.

Step 1: Click on File Explorer, located at the top left corner

Step 2: Choose New Folder

Step 3: Customize the name to your preferred choice

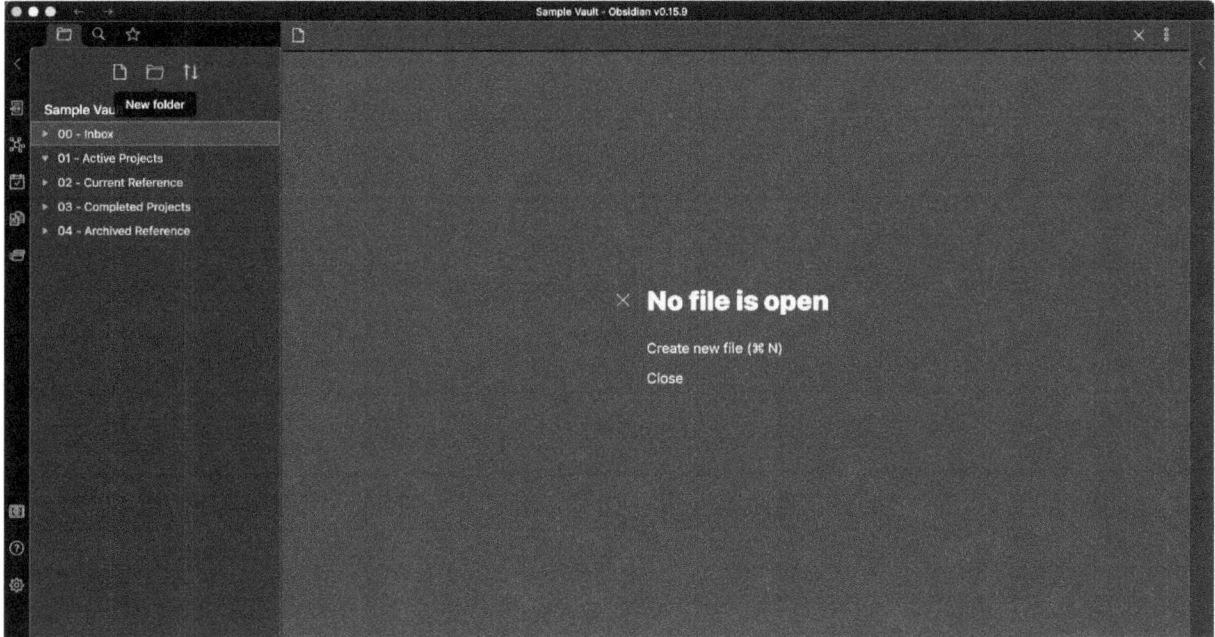

Creating your First Note

As a beginner, you have two simple ways to create a new note automatically. First, you can go a long way by clicking on the File Explorer at the upper left section of the Obsidian interface, then selecting the New Note tab or simply pressing CMD or Ctrl + N on the keyboard.

Most importantly, you can create a link via the App or through a link

Next, put choose a name for your note and save it to your system's local storage as {Chosen-name.md.}

After this, then you can start writing your note. You can apply nested bullets, headers, lists, bullet points and highlights to your texts while formatting.

New Note Via link

When working in Obsidian, one of the unique things that can be done to create a note, to save you time, is to generate a note via a link. It can essentially link to a note that doesn't yet exist. This is fantastic when you're working on a note and realize you'll need to make another note but don't want to fill it out right away. Simply make a new link and give it the name you wish to give the new note.

Sounds complicated? Let's construct an illustration to demonstrate how this functions.

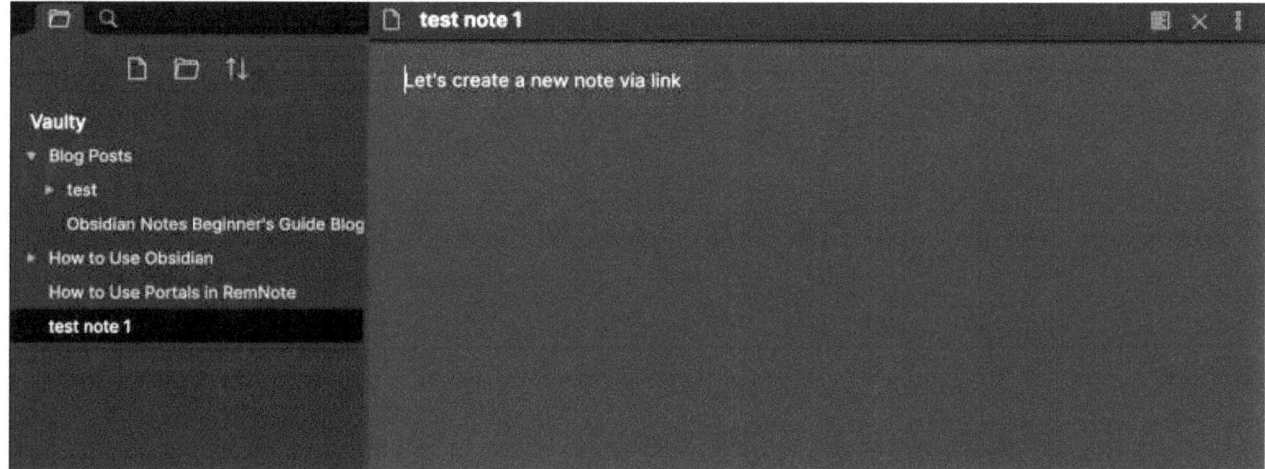

We have a little note up there.

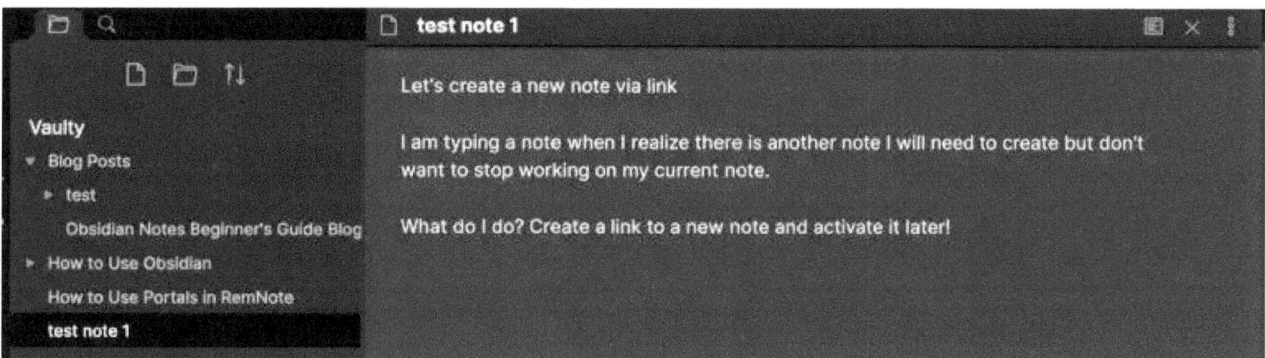

Let's say that while working on your note, you realize you need to make another note. However, you don't want to interrupt what I'm doing. What do you do? When you are prepared to fill out that new note, you can create a new link to a note that doesn't yet exist and activate it.

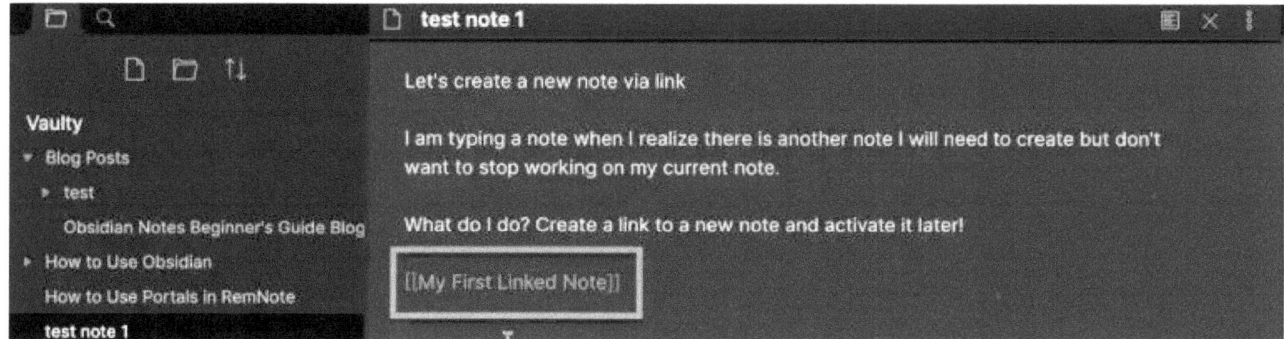

The name of the link or note, two open braces ([[), and two closing braces (]]) are the order in which links are created in Obsidian.

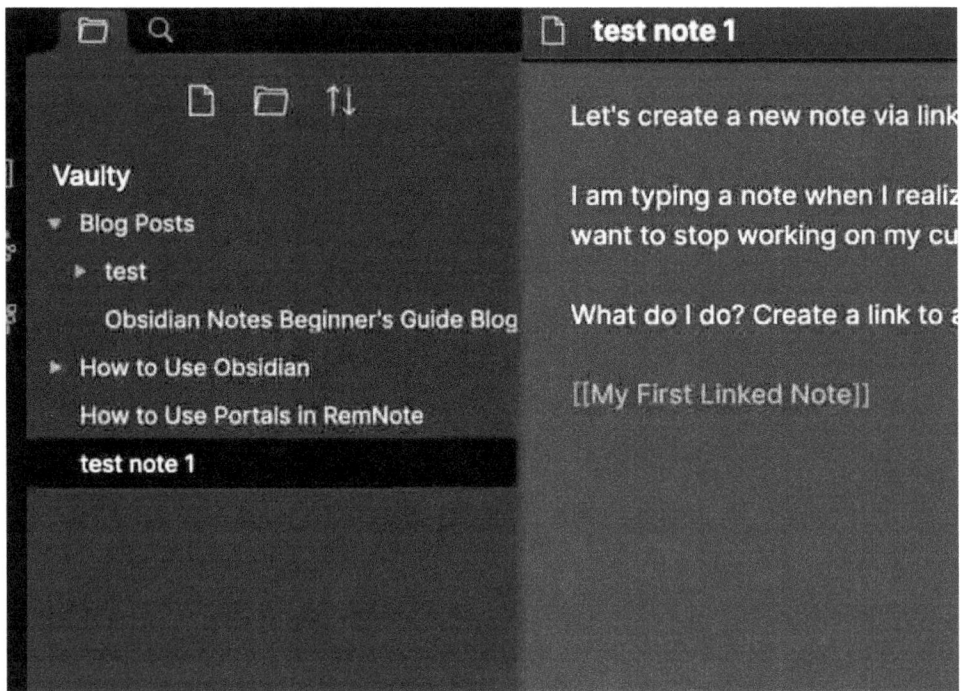

By doing this, a new note that doesn't already exist is linked. Even though the link is in the screenshot above, the note is not shown in the note list on the left. This is so that the link may be created, which requires clicking on it.

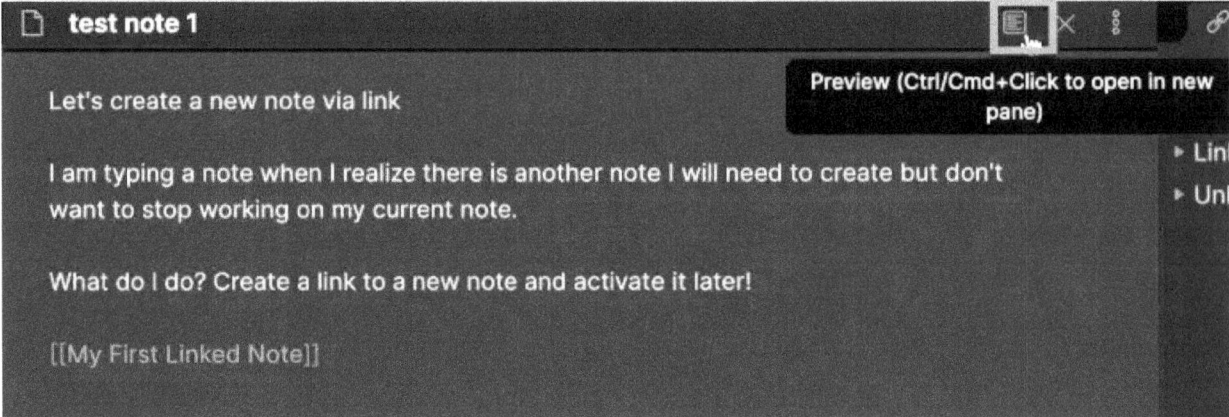

The best way to do that is to click the link after switching the current note's edit mode to preview mode. A button that switches between preview and edit mode is located on the right side of the note's title bar, as shown in the image above. While the preview mode displays the document with the specified formatting, the edit mode allows you to write and amend the document.

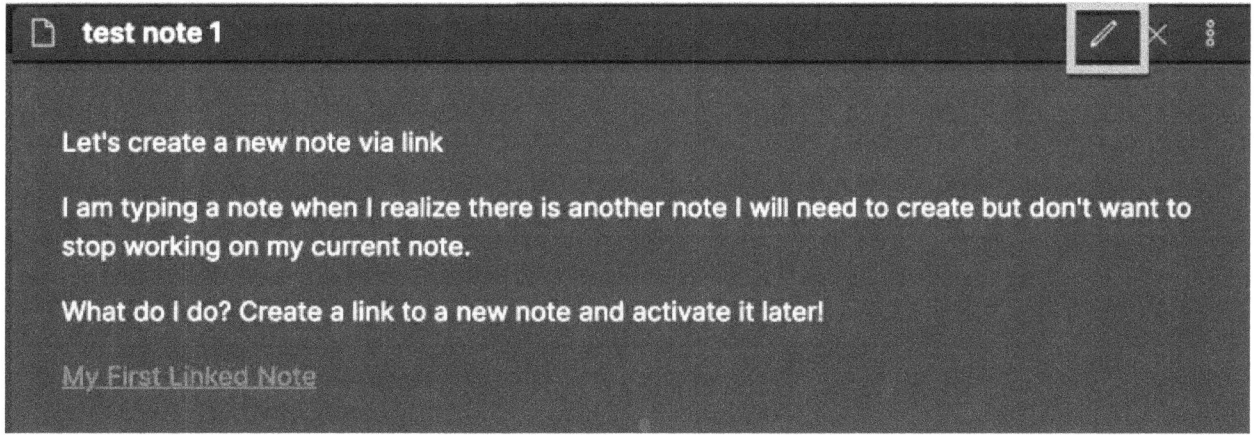

Press the toggle switch. Now, your screen ought to resemble the one seen above. The toggle button had changed to a pencil icon, which, when clicked, returns you to edit mode, and the link no longer has braces. Click the note's link to start a new note now.

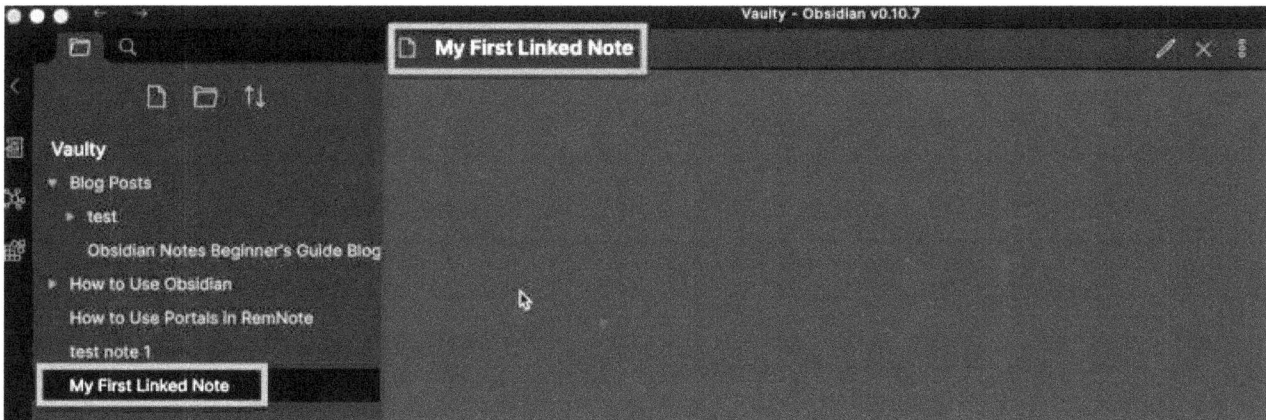

The main window and the notes panel will display your new note. Click the pencil icon to modify your new note, then enter some content.

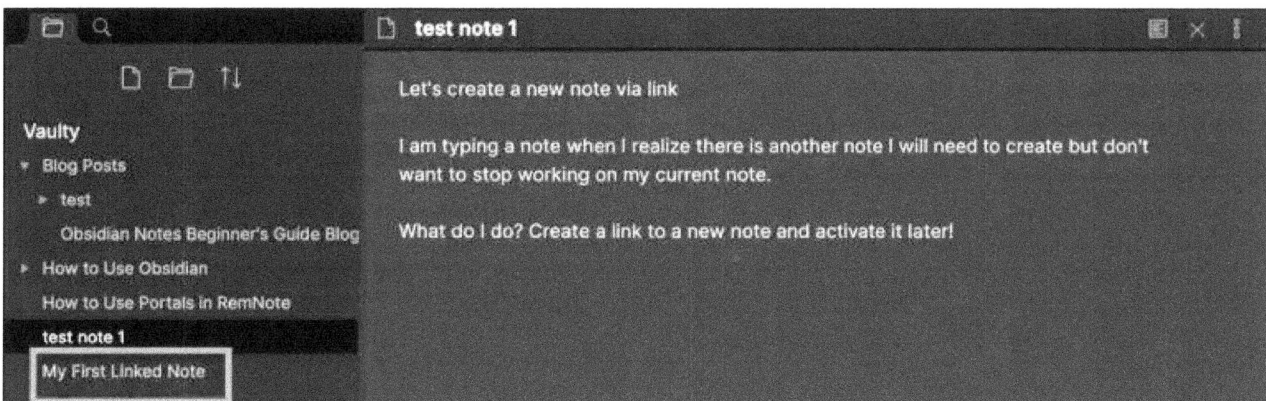

The amazing part is that even if you remove the link from the original page, as displayed above, this document will still be available. This is a lifesaver for me because I regularly have ideas for new notes that I need to write but don't want to stop working on the current note. If you have a project where you know you need specific notes for components of the project, this link strategy also works well. All the necessary documents can be linked to a master project page. Simply click the link when you are ready to fill out those notes.

Organizing Notes

In Obsidian, you may drag and drop your notes into the folder of your choice. You drag the note's title to a folder by clicking and holding the note's title on the left side.

Now that we are done with the Basics; we can address some other important actions you can initiate in the Obsidian App.

How to search for text in a note

Searching for things manually can be daunting, even when you know the name. But it doesn't have to be, the best course of action is normally to check all notes, but that is also very time-consuming.

Let's use Bob Uecher as an example. He has a memorable comment regarding knuckleballs. Let's say you need it and can't recall the exact statement but still know Uecher made it, so this is what comes up when we type "Uec" into Obsidian:

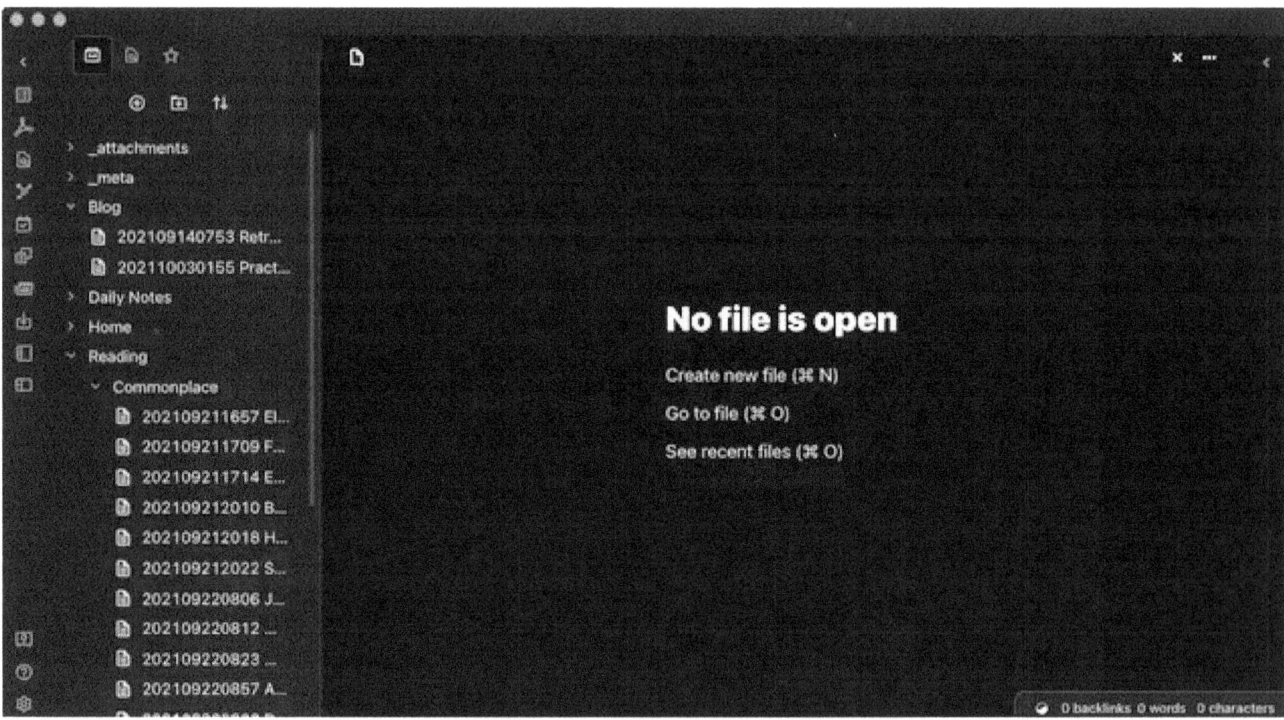

Here is how we got to what you see on the screenshot:

Step 1: Click on the "Search" space.

Step 2: Enter **"uec"** in the search box.

Step 3: Choose the match you wish to show the note for from the search results.

Step 4: The text we searched for was highlighted in yellow in the note, as you can see.

Using Note Dates for Quick Search

Obsidian has the same note-by-date search functionality as Evernote. For these searches, Obsidian uses the file dates. However, you could access Evernote and modify a note's Create date. This was helpful, too, because you might have frequently compared a note's creation date to the date on a document. At this point, you can use a hotkey in Obsidian to identify a note's creation date. However, there is a simpler method, which is why we've included the prefix Zettelkasten format.

Imagine that we wanted to look up every note from October 3, 2021. We need to enter the following into the search bar, assuming you prefix all of your note titles with your Zettelkasten prefix: 20211003:

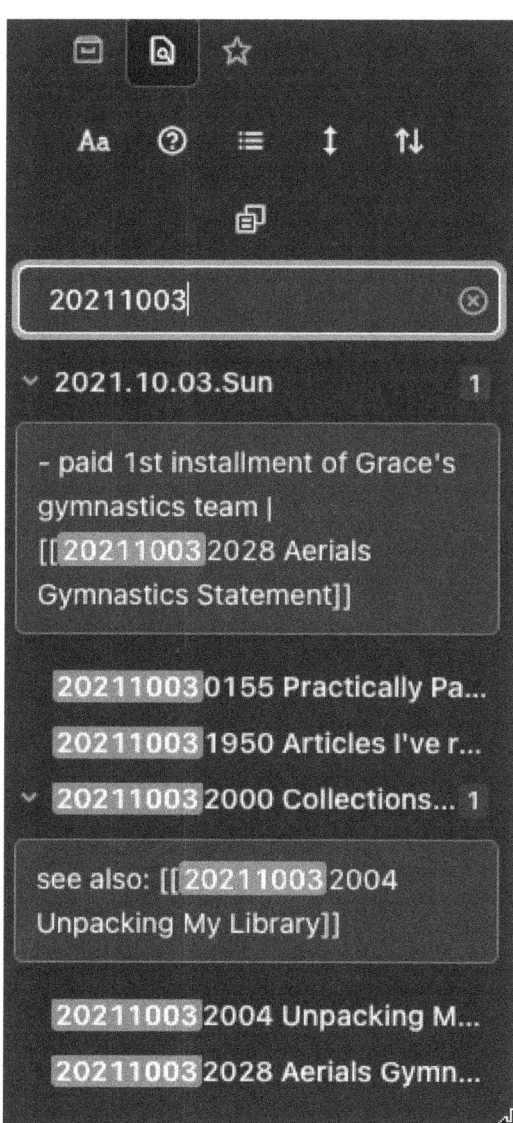

You can see that my search yields six notes with that date as a prefix. A note's contents can be viewed by clicking on it. Notably, one of the matches is the daily entry for October 3, 2021. The note appears in the list of matched notes even though it doesn't have a Zettelkasten prefix since it refers to another note that does.

Note Search with Tags

You can search notes by tag by prefixing my search with "tag:". If you like, you can include many tags in the search. Let's say you wanted to look for any notes with the tags #baseball and #lists. This is how it appears in your Obsidian Vault:

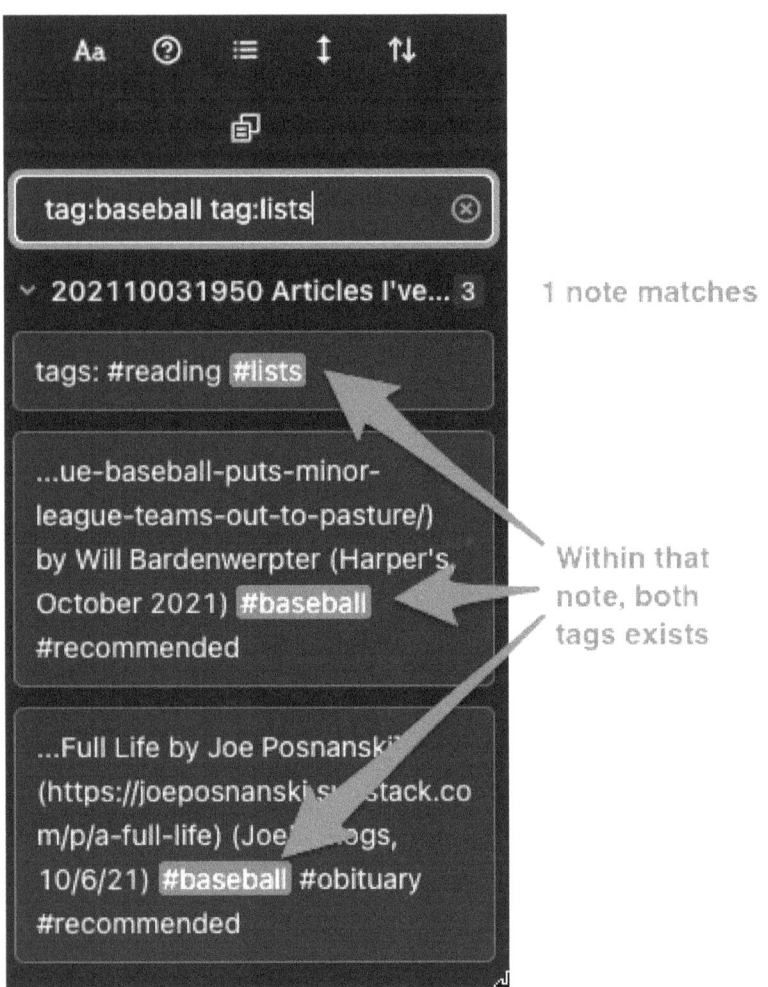

Searching for To-do items

Finally, I can search for tasks based on their status (completed, marked as "to-do," or done, according to Obsidian). Let's say I want to look for any notes from October 2021 that have unfinished business. This is how that search appears in Obsidian:

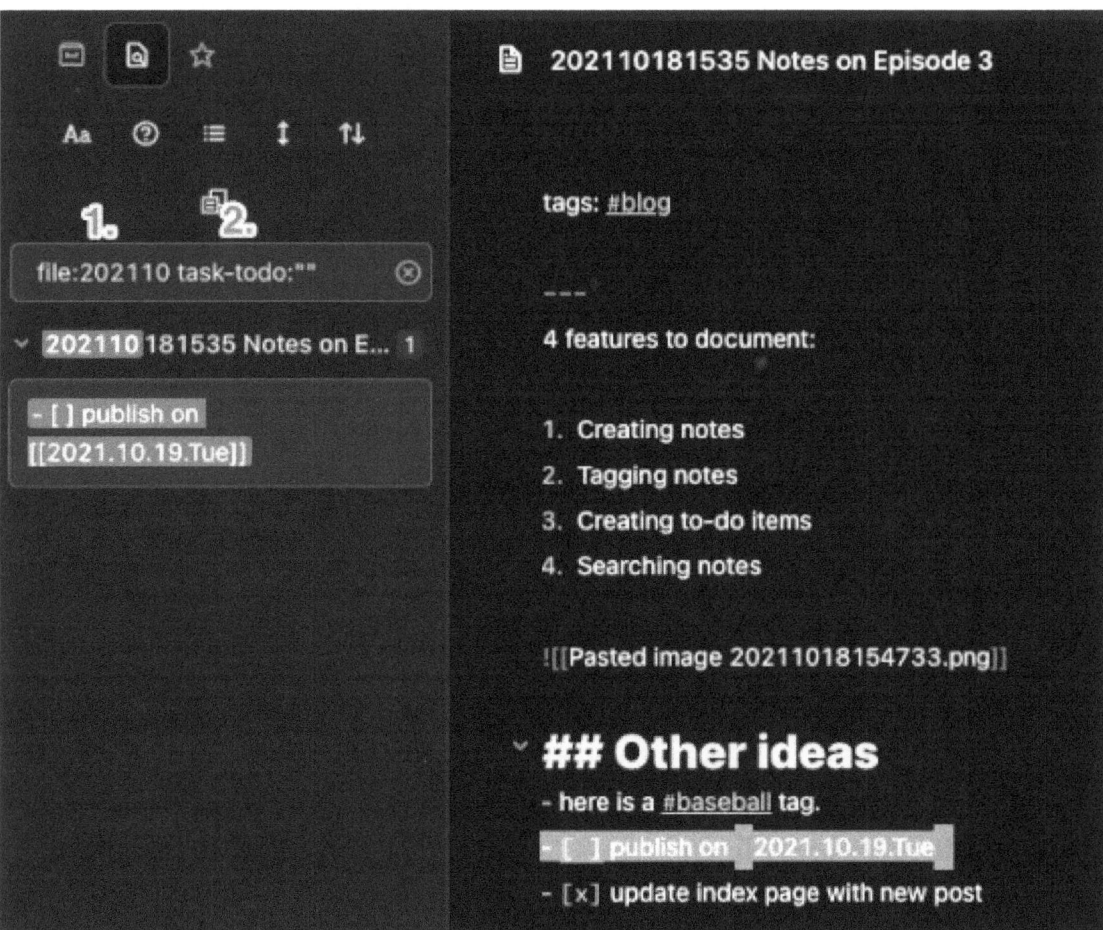

What is happening is as follows:

I'm looking for files with the name 202110, which stands for 2021 (year) and 10 (month).

I'm also looking for any notes that include tasks that aren't finished: task-todo:"

One note is produced as a result—the one I wrote at the start of this piece. The only unfinished work for the month is underlined within the note in yellow, and the note's title begins with the number 202110.

Workspaces

If you're used to using a notepad and pen for note-taking, you will understand that it can be hard at times, especially when you have to find a stage to keep your Notepad or iPad at eye level while working to keep track of your development. That is what the workspace feature seeks to resolve. To carefully curate and organize your workflow.

But first, you must activate the plug-in before initiating the process.

To do this,

Step 1: Go to the Core Plug-in section (Check Core plug-in details to understand how to locate it)

Step 2: Check for Workspaces and click on the slider to turn it (Once activated, you will see the **"Manage workspaces"** button added to the left toolbar.)

Step 3: Click on Exit settings to leave.

Step 4: You can assign a shortcut to Workspace using the create shortcut section.

Once activated, you can now arrange the views and windows you use exactly how you like them and save the arrangement as a custom workspace. Refer to the [[Split-view]] section above to learn what you can do. You can select the preset view by clicking "manage workspaces" when using it again.

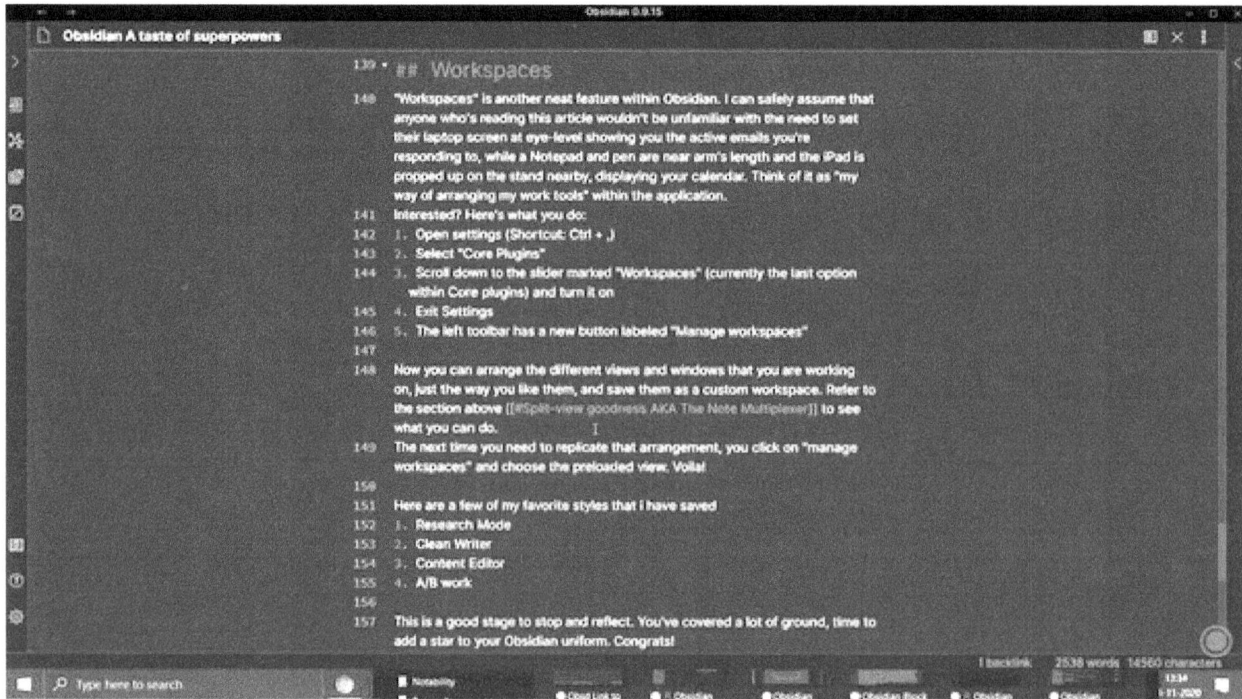

Common Obsidian Styles

Here's an explanation of some useful styles and what they are used for:

Editor Mode

This style is used to review articles and notes. Below is a screenshot of how it looks.

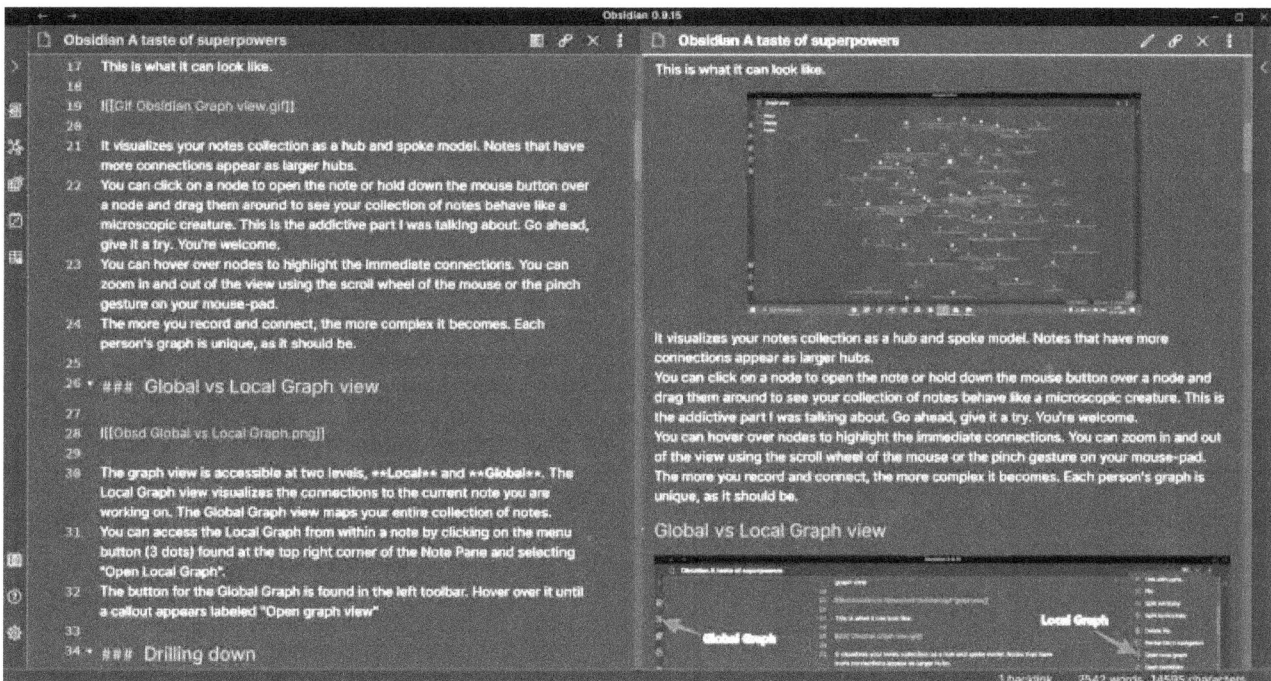

Research Mode

This style is suited for brainstorming. Below is a review of how the interface looks like:

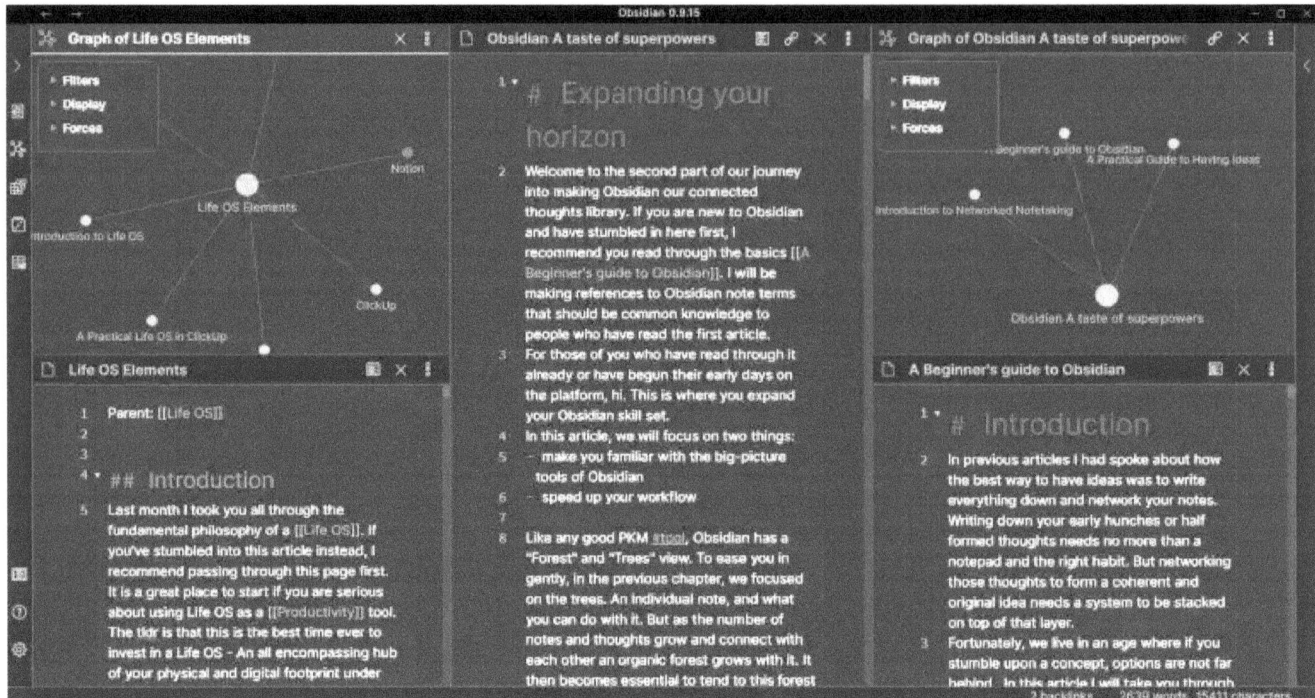

Clean Writer

As the name implies, clean water is a style that is devoid of extra distractions. Used to maintain concentration during in-depth content creation

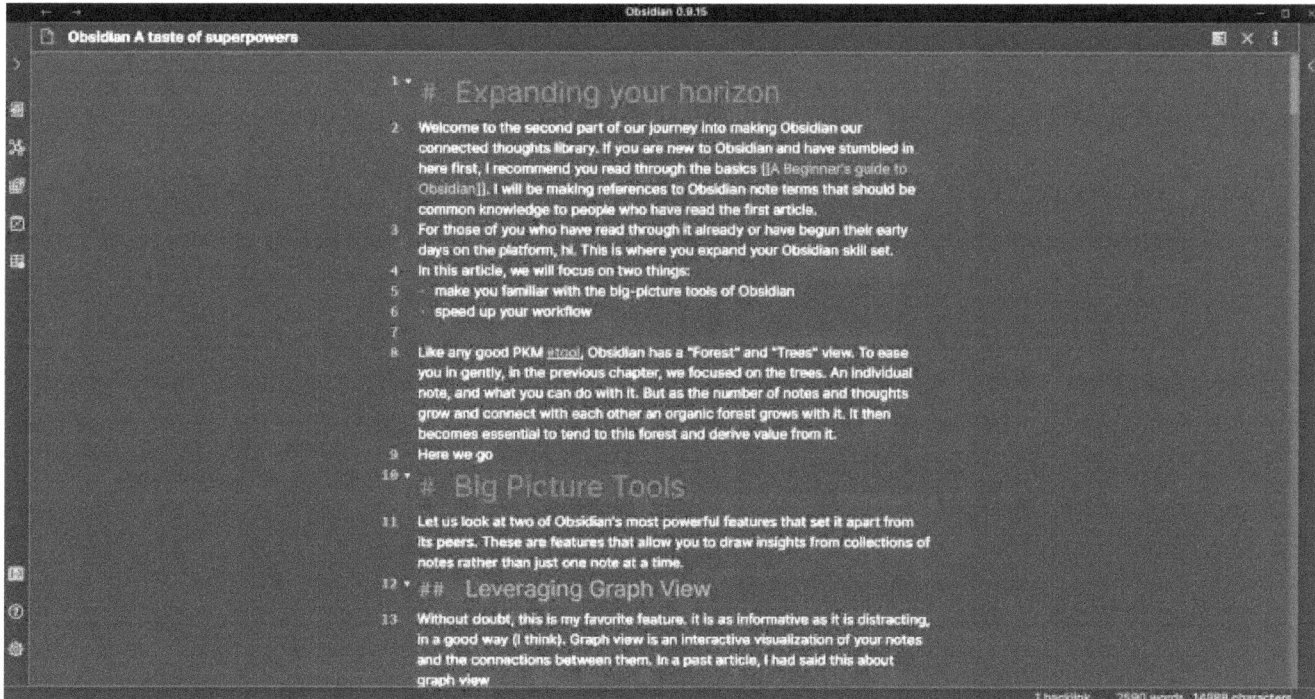

A/B Mode

You can use this style for comparison. It appears handy while checking the difference between two versions of the same notes.

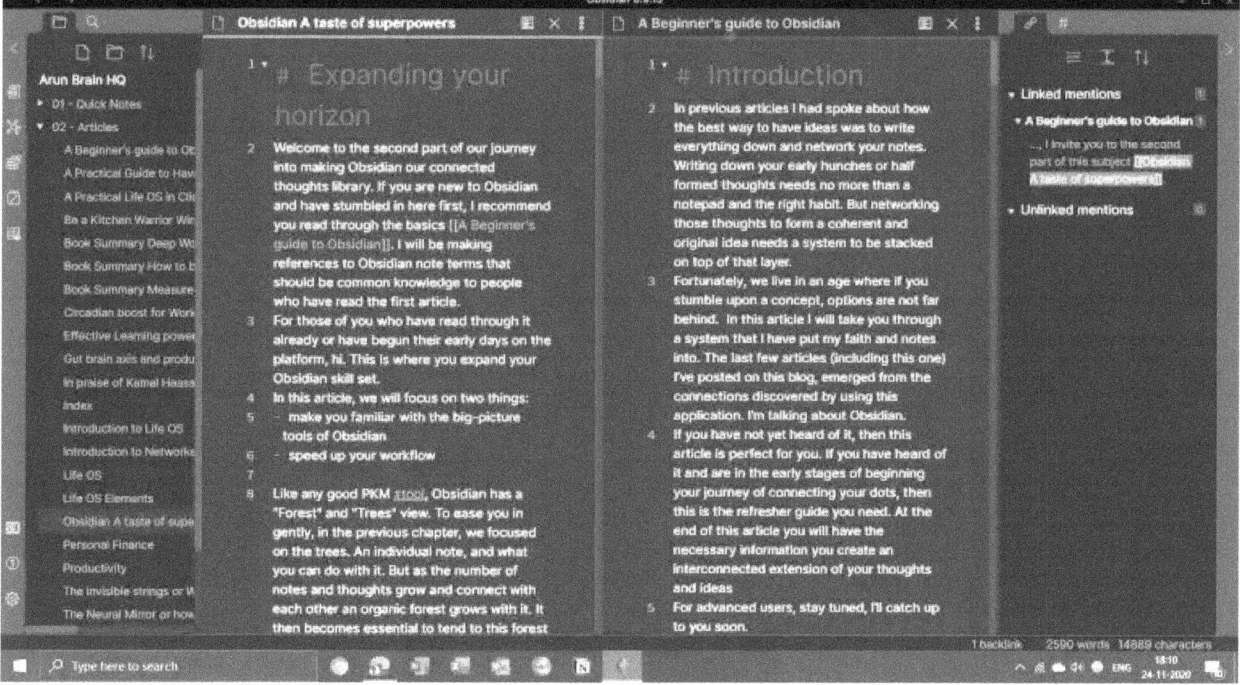

Text Editing

Though we have highlighted some vital text editing shortcuts and basics, It is obvious that formatting texts on Obsidian are different from Notepad and other word processors like MS word. But the fact remains that you need its rich collection of text formatting functionalities, which are mostly available on Markdown.

Obsidian uses Markdown instead for text editing. The markdown syntax enables the use of symbols that can be read as text formatting within the text. Although it seems difficult, we will explain some fundamentals in the section below.

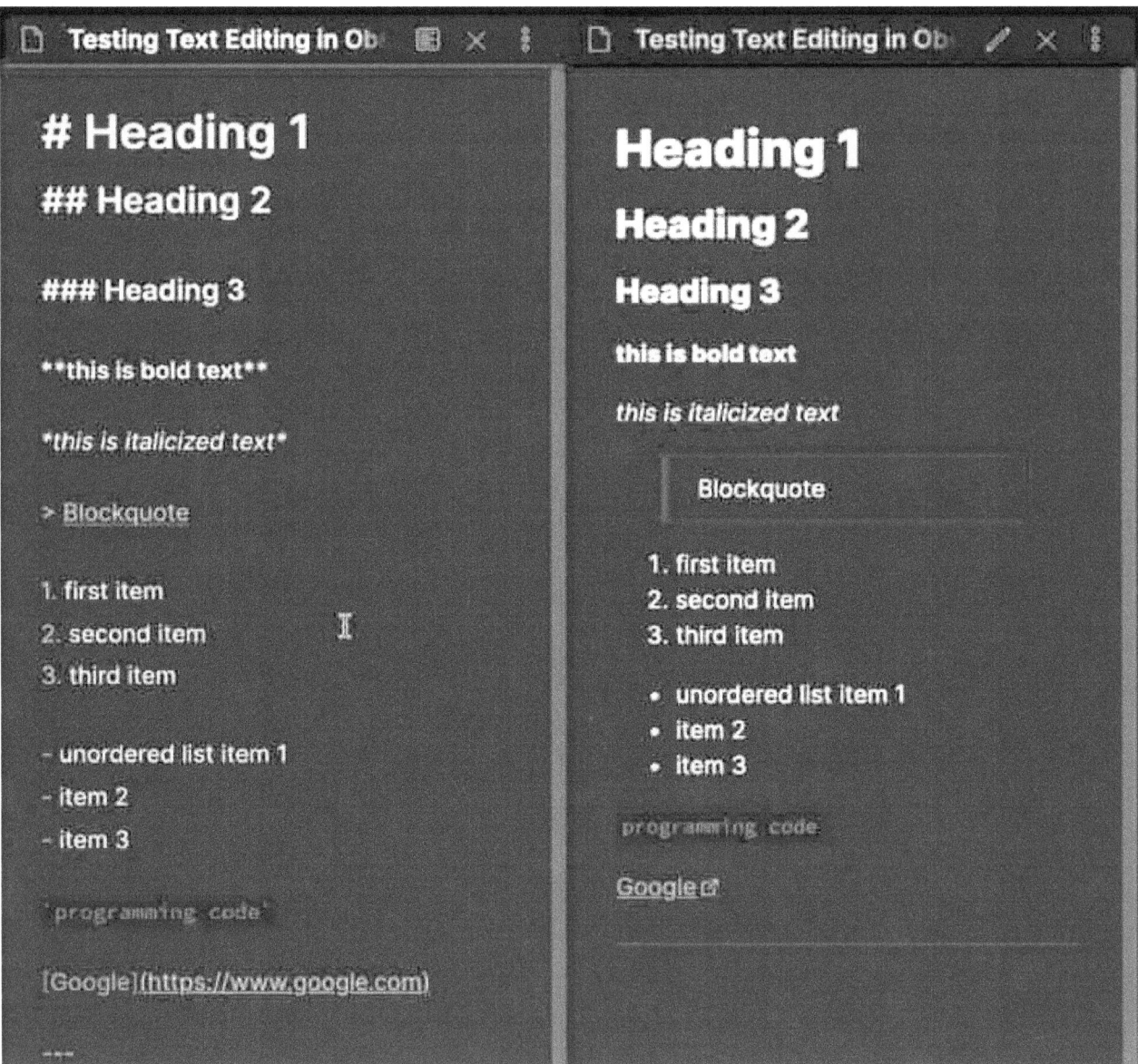

The right-hand pane of the above screenshot demonstrates text formatting, and the left pane shows how it reflects on Markdown writing. It doesn't look so daunting anyways.

Split View

As the name suggests, split view lets you open multiple notes simultaneously. Obsidian achieves this by dividing the window into as many note/graph views as you wish rather than running different tabs simultaneously like in other word processing programs like Microsoft word.

To activate the split view, follow the steps below:

Step 1: You must choose a vertical or horizontal split-screen. So go to the top right pane and click on the three dots, choose either Split horizontally or vertically.

Step 2: Choose either a new graph or a note from the option.

Step 3: Once it opens, you can open a backlink by right-clicking on it ([[backlink]]) and tapping "**Open in a new pane.**"

Step 3: To choose a note in Graph view, hover your cursor over it and then press down **Ctrl** and **click**.

Step 4: You can follow the instructions above to assign a shortcut to your Split view.

The best part is that you can use it in literally any screen size and open up to 4 notes without overworking your system UI menus.

Below is a screenshot of how your screen will look like.

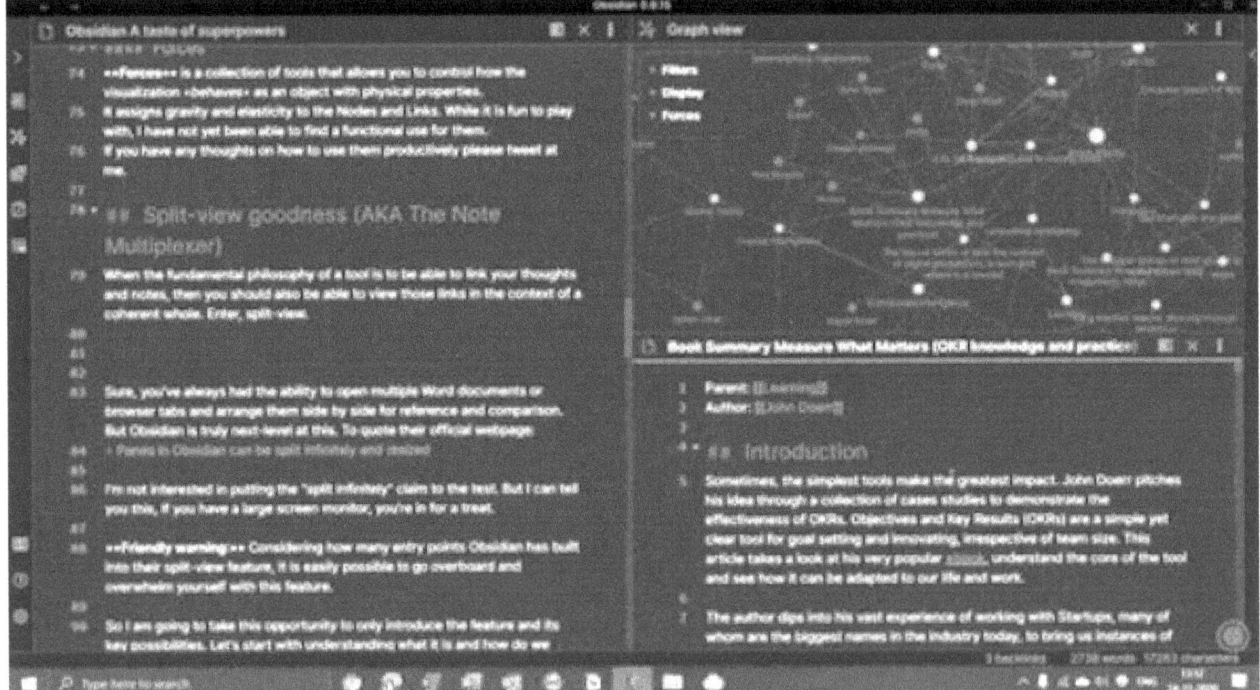

Note: Given the number of access points Obsidian included in their split-view functionality, it is simple to overuse and become overwhelmed by it.

So we will use this chance only to describe the functionality and its main applications. Let's begin by comprehending what it is and how to use it.

Why is a split view important?

The reason for the split view cannot be overemphasized, and frequent users of such an option, like programmers, probably understand how important it is for idealization. However, here are some reasons why you need an Obsidian Split screen.

- Split view is an excellent research tool. Whether you are producing new content or making comments on already published content, nothing beats having the related notes open for quick access to "blocks that can be connected" and "quotes that can be cited to add depth and credibility to your material."
- A split view is useful when working with Content Maps. A different post that examines more advanced Obsidian concepts and applications are necessary to light this meta-note. But for now, content maps might be viewed as a homepage for notes connected to a larger topic.
- Open a blank note and a split-view of its local graph to see the connections you are forming in real-time. This makes it possible for you to tell apart connections that lead to notes that have already been generated from those that point to notes that have yet to be written.
- The split-view might be useful when you create a content mood board for ideas or want to review a tired subject.
- Having two pieces of information open in a single interface gives a distraction-free working environment when you need to examine or compare and contrast them.
- Graph view and Split view are two of Obsidian's unique features that let you address your notes simultaneously. Process optimization is the other thing you should be aware of to advance in Obsidian.

How to Import Files

You can import any kind of file, but as a beginner, we can restrict this to the main files you would be working with, which include audio, videos, images, and PDFs. However, you must confirm that the content is in the vault folder. Creating an attachments folder and storing all of your media is a common practice. Once your material is in the obsidian folder, you can connect to it using the following syntax:

Importing Images

There are two ways to import images into your note; first, you can drag and drop or use Markdown syntax. The following image file formats can be imported into your Obsidian note: PNG, JPG, JPEG, GIF, BMP, and SVG

Drag the image into the note interface

Once you drag and drop, Obsidian automatically puts the imported file in the attachment folder. But I suggest you create a folder to make your note idea easy to comprehend and less clumsy.

Below is a step-by-step process on how to drag and drop your image

Step 1: Add a pane with the same note in preview mode after opening your note in edit mode.

Step 2: Open an image in your local file storage

Step 3: Drag the image into the edit mode of the note

Step 4: As seen in the screenshot below, the preview pane should display the image, while the edit mode pane should display the markdown image syntax.

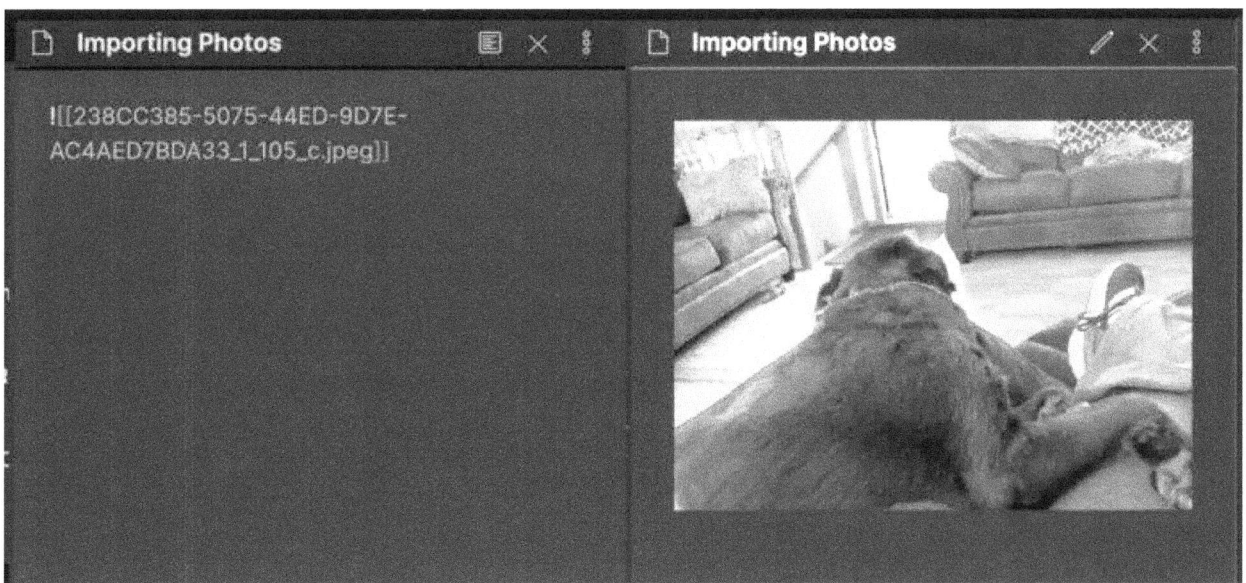

Use Markdown syntax

The best part of using Obsidian is that the syntaxes are pretty simple to memorize. So if you want to add an image file with the file format at the end. Let 's say you want to add an image saved with Bexy saved in jpg; you will need to put the syntax like this, **[Image](Bexy. jpg)**

To adjust the file size, you can type the dimension in pixels into an open and closed bracket "()."

Importing Audio and Videos

Obsidian allows you to also import videos and audio by dragging and dropping into the note interface; you just need to drag into the edit mode and then see the result in the preview pane, as shown in the screenshot below. For audio, the compatible file formats include, Mp3, WebM, WAV, M4a, Ogg, 3gp, and FLAC; on the other hand, video files include, Mp4, WebM, and ogv.

Importing PDFs

The procedure seems almost the same with all the media files but tends to be slightly different with PDF files. Since PDFs cannot be physically included in the notes, so they will have to appear as attachments. This means that you will not see your actual PDF file but a preview of the title of your file in preview mode.

You will see a box with an arrow on the bottom left. On hovering the cursor over it, you will see a notification, Open in Default App. Once you click, your PDF file will automatically open with your computer's default PDF reader.

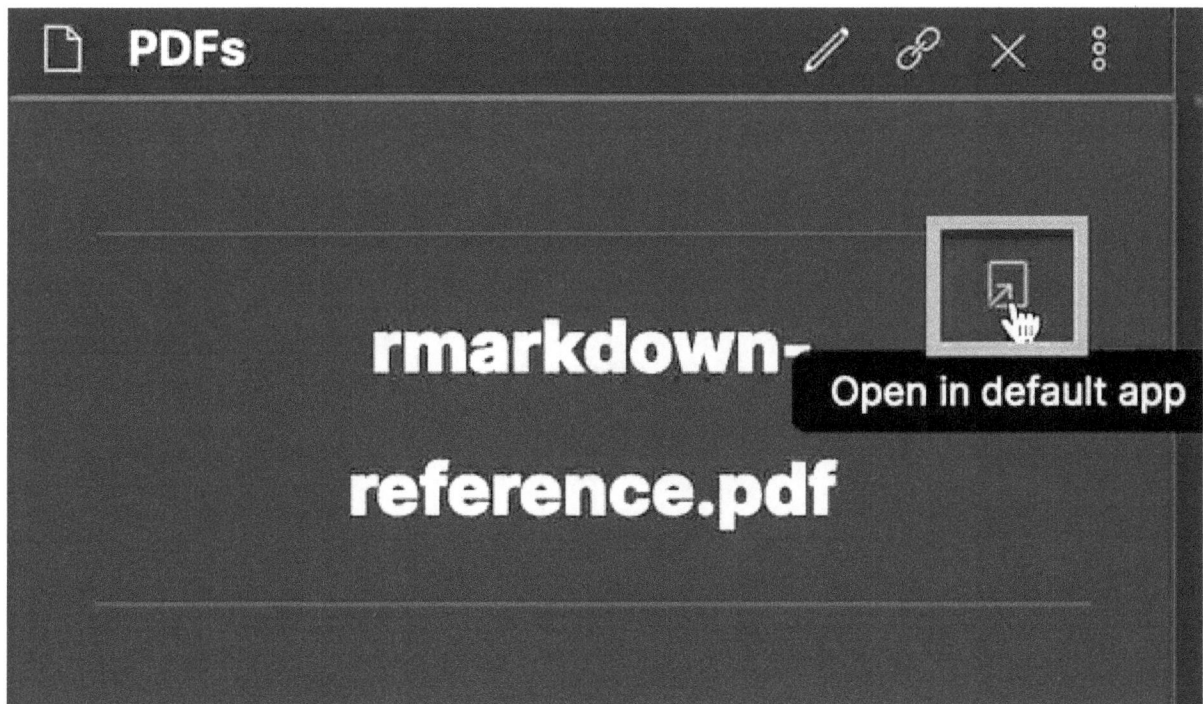

Knowledge Graph

Anytime you press CTRL + G, Obsidian's graph will take the place of your active note. The graph visually displays the connections and tags among your notes, assisting you in discovering relationships between notes you weren't previously aware of.

Using knowledge graphs is an excellent way to see how the different notes in your Vault are connected. When first using Obsidian, this might not seem like a big deal. The knowledge graph will reveal more and more linkages, some of which may not be immediately obvious, as you add more and more notes and backlinks to link information together.

There are two tiers of the graph view: local and global. The connections to the note you are working on are displayed in the Local Graph view. The Global Graph view displays a map of all of your notes.

By selecting **"Open Local Graph"** from the menu button (three dots) in the top right corner of the Note Pane, you can access the Local Graph from within a note.

The left toolbar contains the Global Graph button. When an **"Open graph view"** callout displays, hover over it.

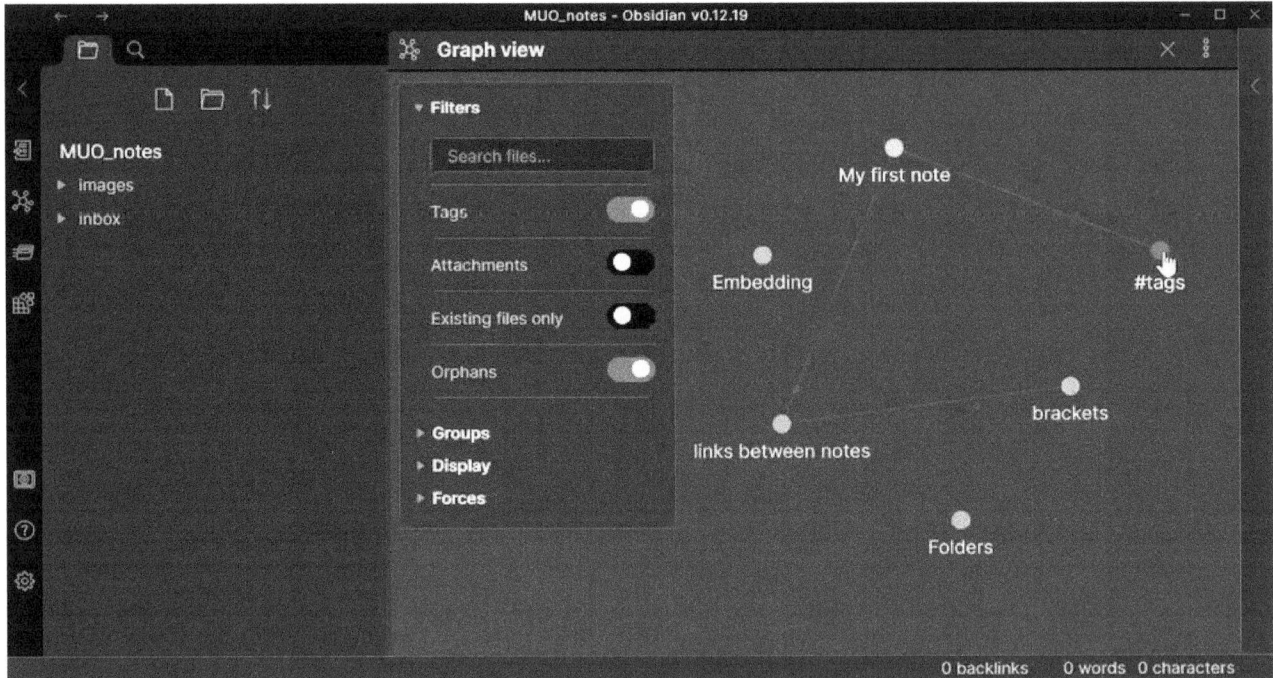

Filtering Knowledge Graphs

Filtering the Knowledge Graph is very straightforward, but you will have to do it with respect to the criteria below:

- It can be used to specify the word count in the note.
- To identify if the note contains tags or not
- If there are attachments or not
- Whether or not the note is tagged
- To specify which notes are existing files, not just links
- If the note is a standalone file with no backlinks to other notes

These features are activated once you toggle the on and off button

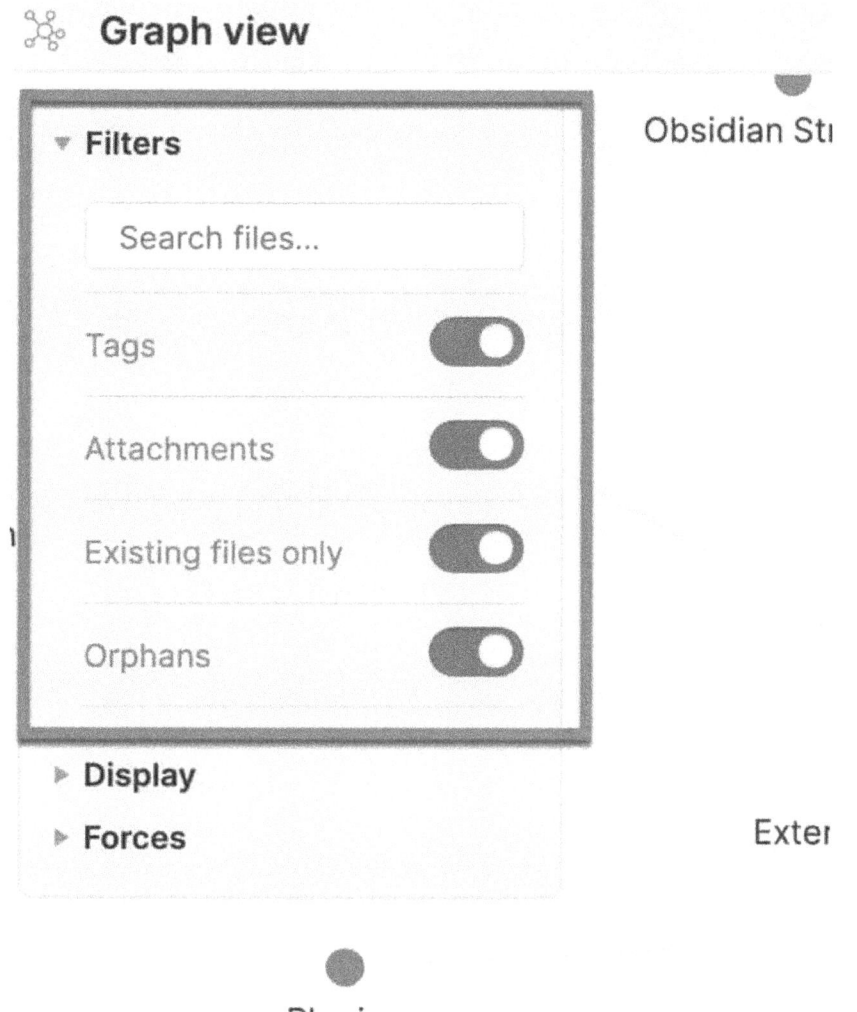

Graph View Details

The graph view is a dynamic representation of your notes and the relationships among them. It depicts the organization of your notes as a hub and spoke design. Larger hubs represent more connected notes.

You can drag a node around the screen while holding the mouse button to see your collection of notes behave like a microscopic creature, or you can click on a node to view the note.

Hovering over nodes will highlight any nearby connections. You can enlarge and reduce the view by using the mouse scroll wheel or the pinch gesture on your mouse pad.

It gets more complicated the more you connect and record. The graph of each individual is distinct, as it should be.

However, it can be accessed on both a local and global level. The connections to the current note you are working on are shown in the Local Graph view. The Global Graph view displays a map of all of your notes.

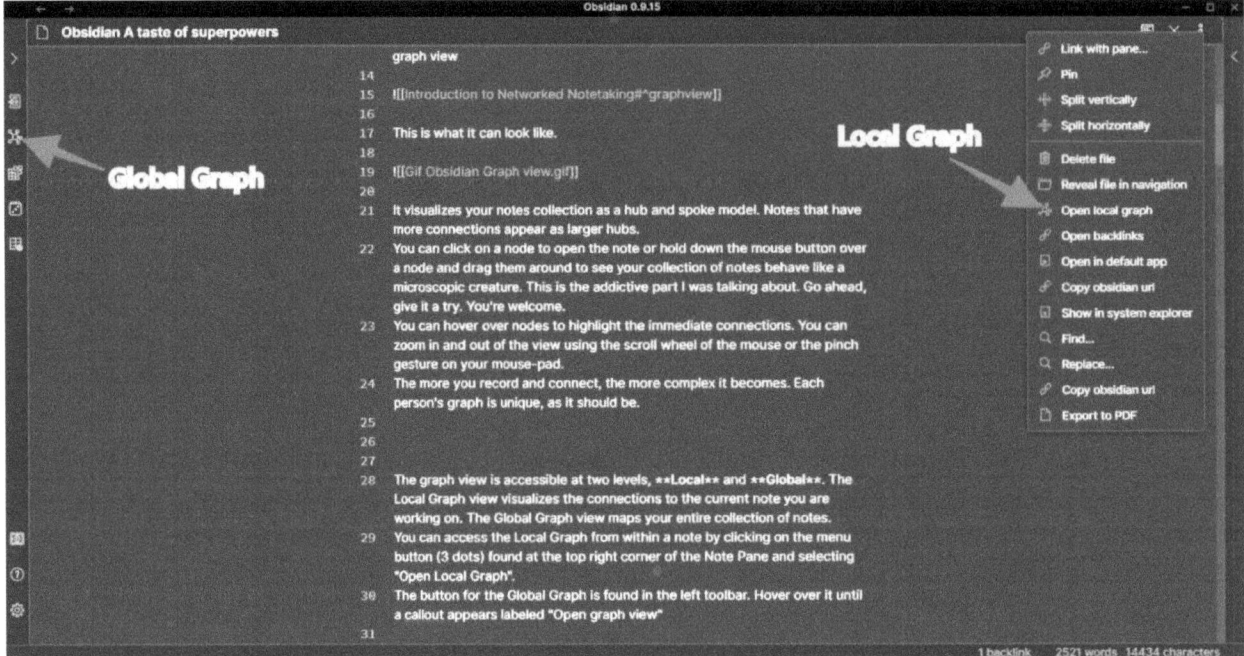

Drilling down

The graph view gives you more precise control over your display, whether you select the Local or Global option. Let's discuss what they do and, more importantly, how you can benefit from using them.

A floating window containing tool options will appear in the top left corner when you open the graph view. Obsidian version 0.9.11 currently has three main controls: Forces, Display, and Filters. They are dropdown menus that cover the applicable controls. It goes like this:

Filters

Filters are one of the most effective tools for generating insights inside your collection since it lets you play with the breadth and depth of the links between notes.

A few different options from the Local and Global views are displayed via the Filters option. We'll talk about them all.

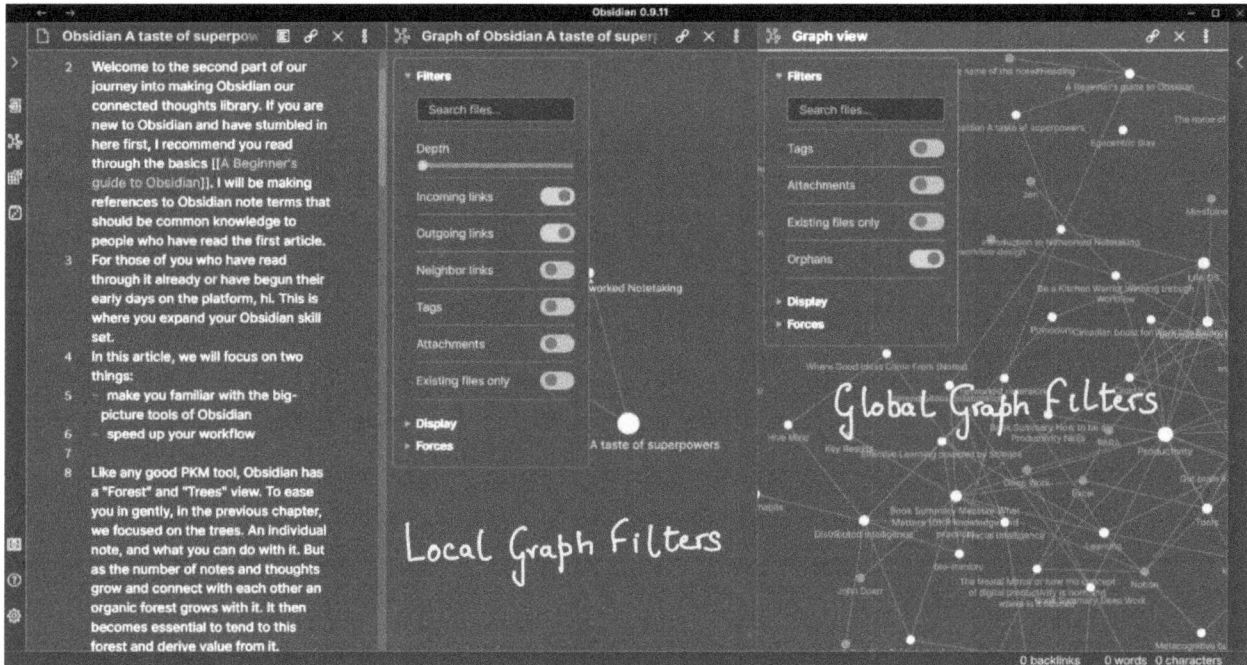

Common Filters

Search

At the top of the menu is "Search", which allows you to filter down to notes containing the search term.

This has many other use cases, too; a powerful example is to use it to search for any missed mentions within notes than can be shepherded into the cluster using backlinks. Another suggestion would be to create easy copy-paste Content Maps.

Standard Toggles

Common toggles allow you to show or hide Tags, Attachments and Existing Files only. That last option mentioned above excludes empty or placeholder notes generated when you create a backlink to a note that does not exist yet or has no content.

Global Graph Extras

Orphans

This toggle points to standalone notes that do not connect to the rest of your collection.

This presents a good opportunity to review them. Decide if they have a connection that needs to be made manually through backlinks or if they are the beginning of a new node where related thoughts and ideas are yet to be recorded.

Local Graph Extras

Depth

This slider control lets you decide what level of separation from your current note you want to see.

If you are working on a tight article on a narrow subject, then you would not go beyond the first level of connection. Still, if you are doing free-form research or fishing for ideas, you will slide over to the 2nd, 3rd or even 4th level of connections to see if there are distantly related topics that spark your brain.

External and Internal Links

These toggles let you view the nature of the connection between the related notes. Combine this with the "Arrows" toggle under Display settings, and the relationship becomes clearer.

One example of where this is useful is in establishing topics where there is a linear flow of logic or a cause-effect relationship between concepts.

Interlinks

This can be turned on to reveal if the disparate topics within the Local Graph are interlinked.

Display

As the name suggests, this collection of tools allows you to control how the visualization looks.

This includes the "Arrows" toggle, which displays the direction in which the notes are linked. If they are bi-directional links, then you see a double-headed arrow.

"Text Fade Threshold" allows you control over text visibility when you zoom in or out

"Node size" and "Link thickness" sliders are obvious labels and need only minor experimentation before you decide what suits your needs

Forces

Force is a collection of tools that allows you to control how the visualization behaves as an object with physical properties.

It assigns gravity and elasticity to the Nodes and Links. While it is fun to play with, it might be hard to get a functional use for them now.

Using YAML in your Obsidian App

YAML is an acronym that means "Yet another markup language." However, it can be used to add metadata to an Obsidian note. This data might be aliases or simple tags. Because YAML is concealed in notes, you can add much information to the markup without cluttering your notes.

This is what a YAML looks like in an Obsidian note:

---

alias: [Top 10 Obsidian blueprint,why Obsidian is the best]

tags: [note,image]

If you have correctly inserted the YAML into your notes, the dashes will change color (by default, they are green).

Obsidian, by default, accepts the YAML files listed below in this order:

alias \tags \cssclass

More YAML metadata can be added, but Obsidian does not natively support it. However, this can still be useful if you're utilizing plug-ins like Dataview.

How to embed pages in Obsidian?

While using Obsidian, you will understand that really; it is important to have a feature like page embedding because of its role in ensuring the ideas are organized with the right connection since it helps you see all the pages in one. This means that once the content on the original page is updated, it gets updated anywhere else it is embedded.

You can link to other pages or blocks around the Obsidian App. And you might even have other unique applications.

If you want to link a single page, use the:

![[Page Name]]

Also, if you want to embed just a paragraph, you can use the same syntax, but you'll need to include the "^" symbol after the page name like so:

![[Page Name^block to link to]]

Also, you can link headings as well as the contents therein. To that, type:

![[Page Name#heading to link to]]

Queries and Search

You can use queries to search your Vault for several notes that meet a given set of requirements. This is useful if you want to make a hub for particular notes. You might tag all notes derived from videos, for instance, and then query your Vault to display only the notes from a particular creator:

If I import the syntax below in my Vault, this will show notes on Images created by Ben Jonas

```
```query
#images + Ben Jonas
```
```

Search

Similarly, if you want to search through previous notes in your Vault, you can do this by using these steps.

On the keyboard, use the shortcuts Ctrl+Shift+F for Windows or Cmd+Shift+F for Mac. Alternatively, select the File Explorer tab and click the "Search" button in the upper left corner.

Links, Tags, and Backlinks

One of the strengths of Obsidian is its powerful implementation of linking. The most basic way to link in Obsidian is the wiki-style link. This is an in-text link to another page in your obsidian vault. You can achieve this by using square brackets like so: [[Page Link]]

You can also link to specific blocks by adding a "^" symbol after your page name, like so: [[Page Link^block to link to]]. When you do this, Obsidian will bring up a context menu to assist you in choosing the correct block in your document. You can link to other pages in your obsidian vault, or you can use this to link to blocks in the current document. This helps create page content for large documents.

You can also link to specific heading by doing this [[Page Link#The Heading]]. However, you can include a plain link at each stage, which, when hovered over, shows a preview. Alternatively, you might embed it by prefixing it with "!" Doing so will add the pertinent extract to your existing note.

We already know how to create new notes via a link, but you can also create:

- Backlinks to specific headers inside a specific document
- Backlinks to other documents
- External links

These link syntaxes are initiated in the Edit Mode. However, the Preview Mode shows how they will appear in your note.

Internal Links

By starting a new note and including the title inside double brackets, you can link to an earlier one. However, one of Obsidian's superpowers allows you to create links to notes that do not yet exist. If a note with that name doesn't already exist when you attempt to open a sentence enclosed in double brackets, Obsidian will create it.

Obsidian works exactly like any other note-taking tool, but it also allows you to link your notes using the equivalent of wikilinks by enclosing them in double square brackets.

You can use aliases to change how links look while previewing a note. For that, insert the pipe character (|) right after your link, followed by the alternative text.

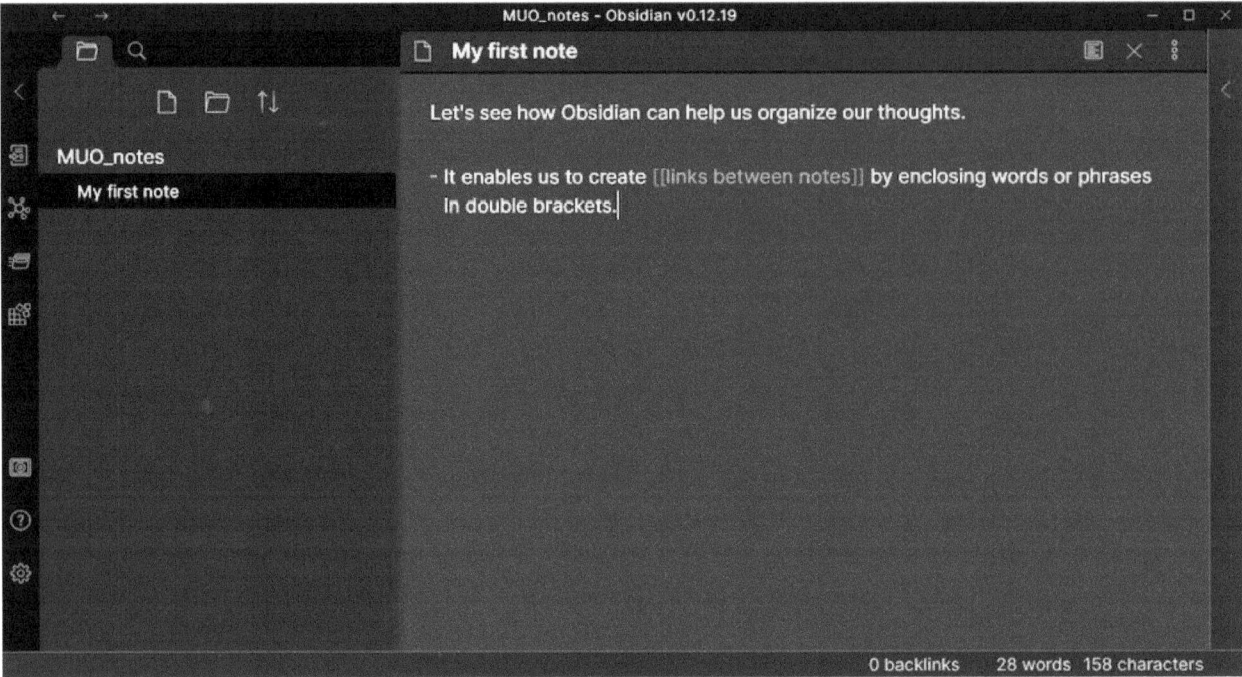

For styling your notes with headings, quotations, and other elements, use Obsidian's full markdown syntax support. Use the normal CTRL + E key sequence to switch between editing and preview mode at any time. This is especially helpful if you want to see a sample of your note in Office, Google Docs, or even WordPress after exporting it.

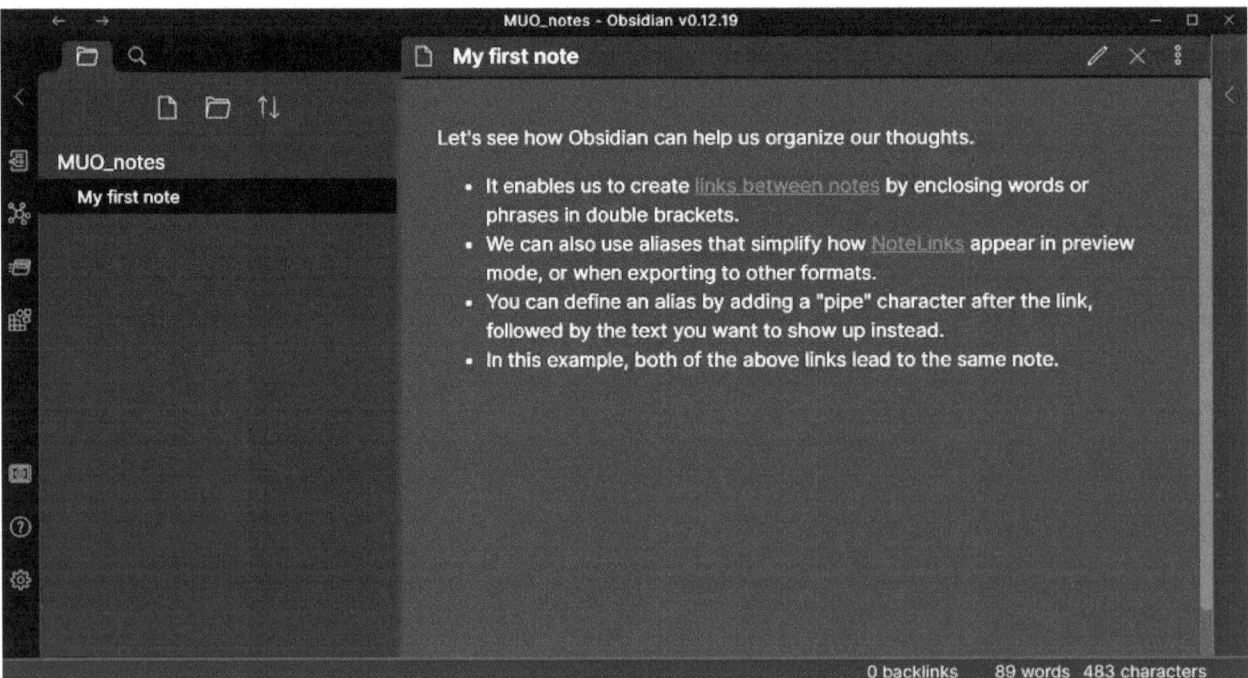

Backlinks

Backlinks are connections between notes that lead to other notes in your Vault. As you link to more notes, everything that connects back to the active note is displayed in the Backlinks window on the right sidebar.

The fact that Obsidian can identify occurrences of a note's name even when they aren't actual links is yet another fantastic feature. In the Backlinks window, you may search for everything that has anything to do with the active note. Backlinks are important for two of these reasons:

- Easy access to relevant content
- Knowledge Graph visualization of the links between notes

However, below is an explanation of how to backlink in Obsidian.

Step 1: Open the note in which you want to create the backlink.

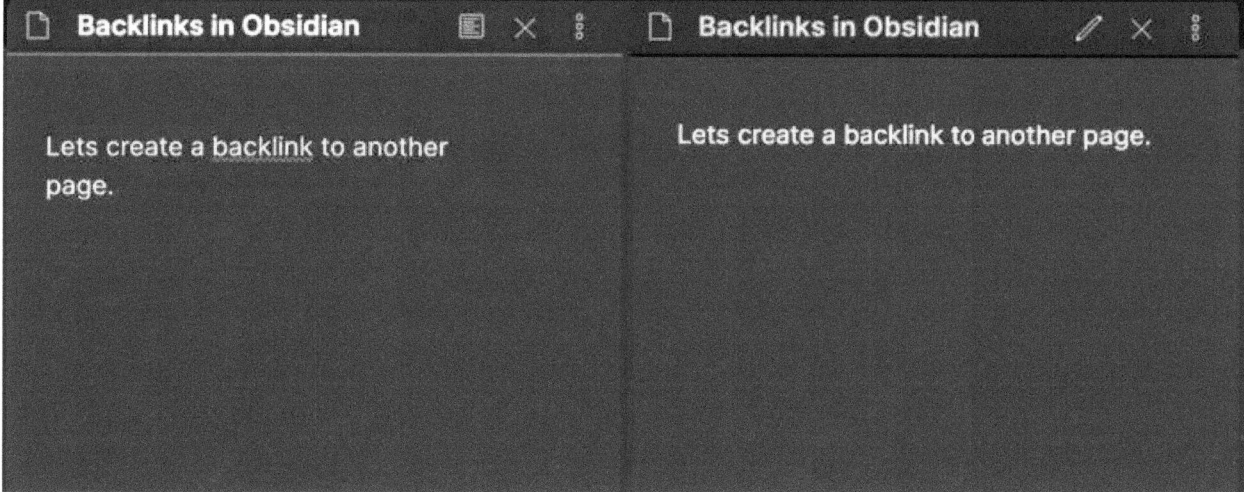

Step 2: Type two open braces to bring up to note selector and select your note from the list

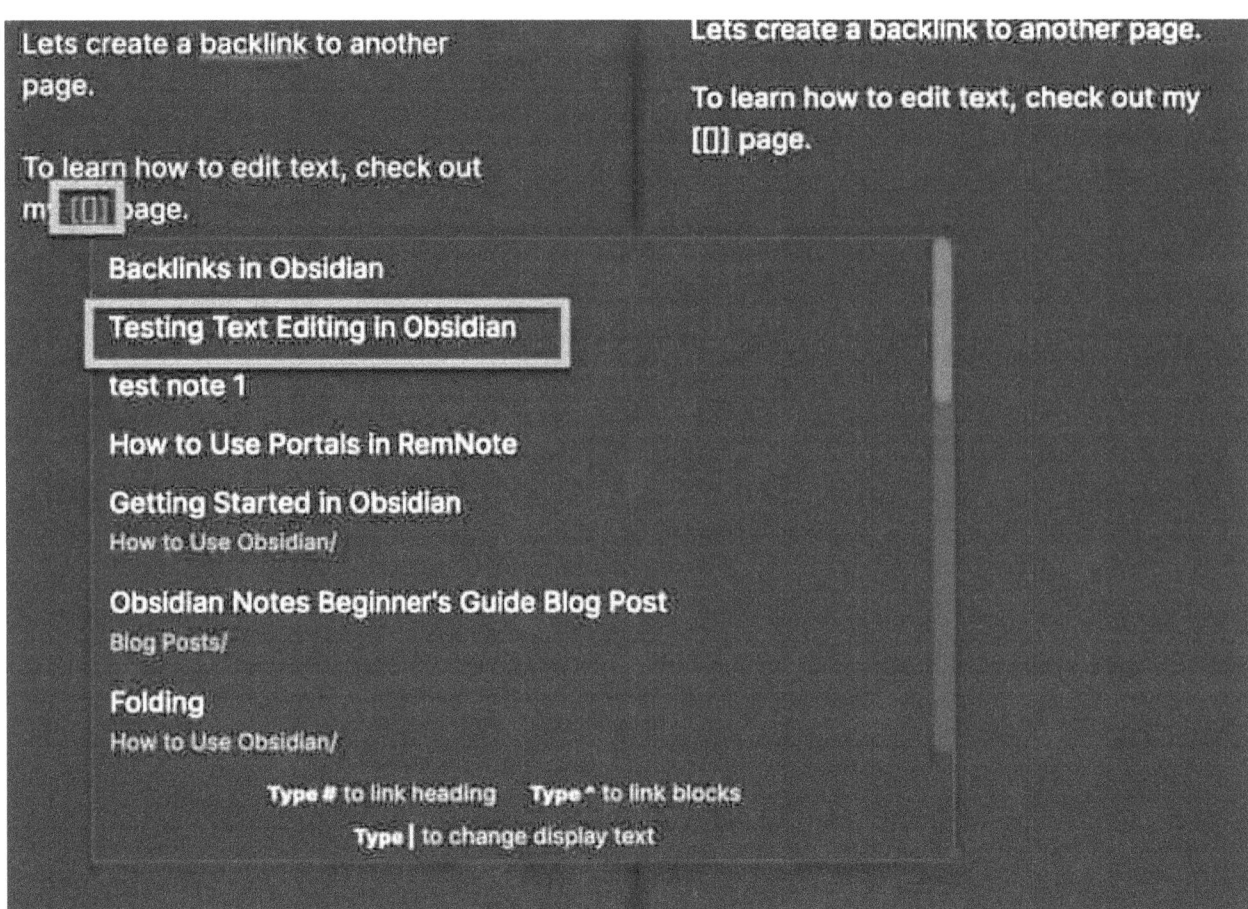

Step 3: Your backlink will now be created

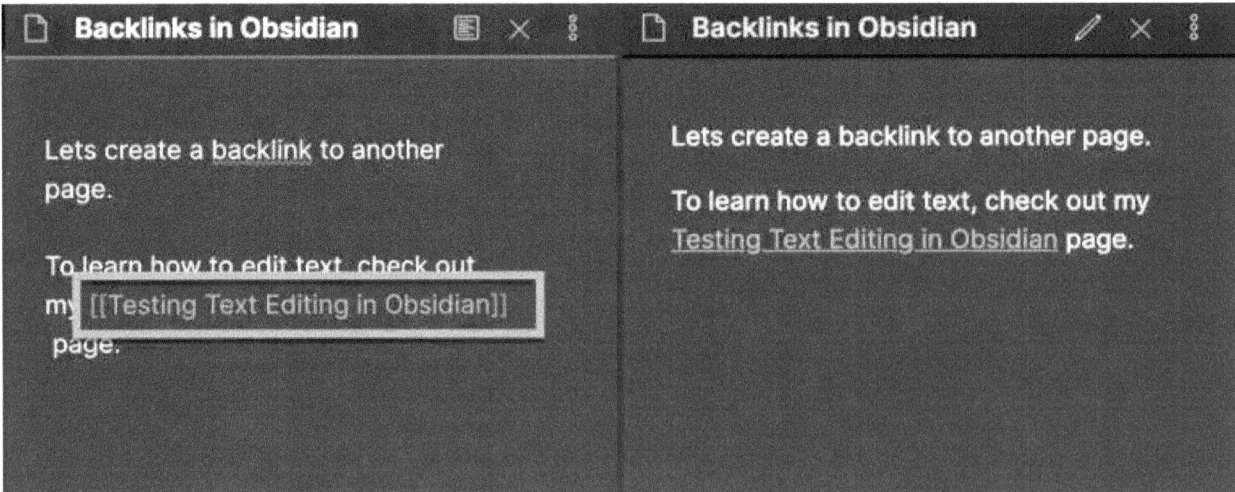

But what if you want to create a link to a specific section of another note? Obsidian supports this as well.

Tags

You can also use tags to organize your notes. However, unlike most note-taking solutions, Obsidian follows the Twitter approach: you can type your tags anywhere you wish.

Some prefer keeping their tags separate from the "main" text, adding them all on a single line. Others find including them in the text "more organic".

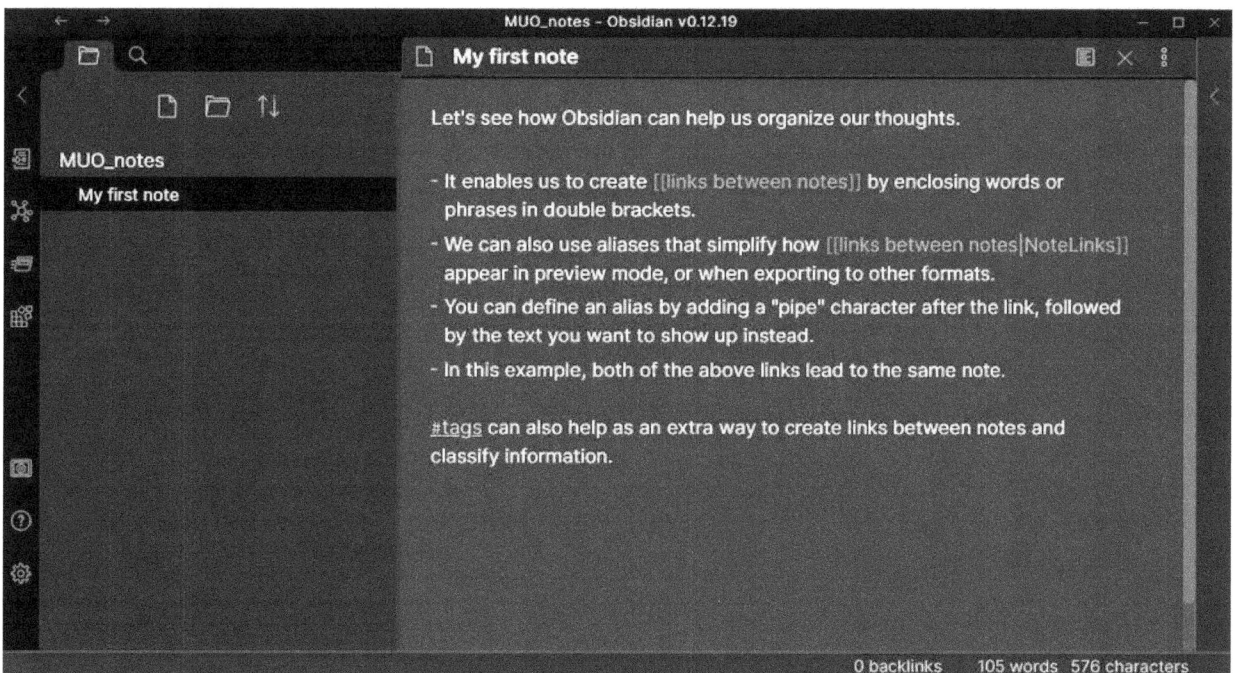

Thus, both of the following approaches are valid:

#muo #note #obsidian

This is my first #note in #obsidian, thanks #muo!

Scanning documents into Obsidian

Earlier, we discussed importing and embedding files; this section will discuss how to scan documents and use them in your Obsidian App. For this practice, we will be using Fujitsu ScanSnap S1300i. This process is compatible with most new-age scanning applications; however, this allows you to scan directly into a vault. Below are the procedures to activate the process:

Step 1: Adjust the configuration

First, you must adjust the application configuration to scan the folder. Check the screenshot to see:

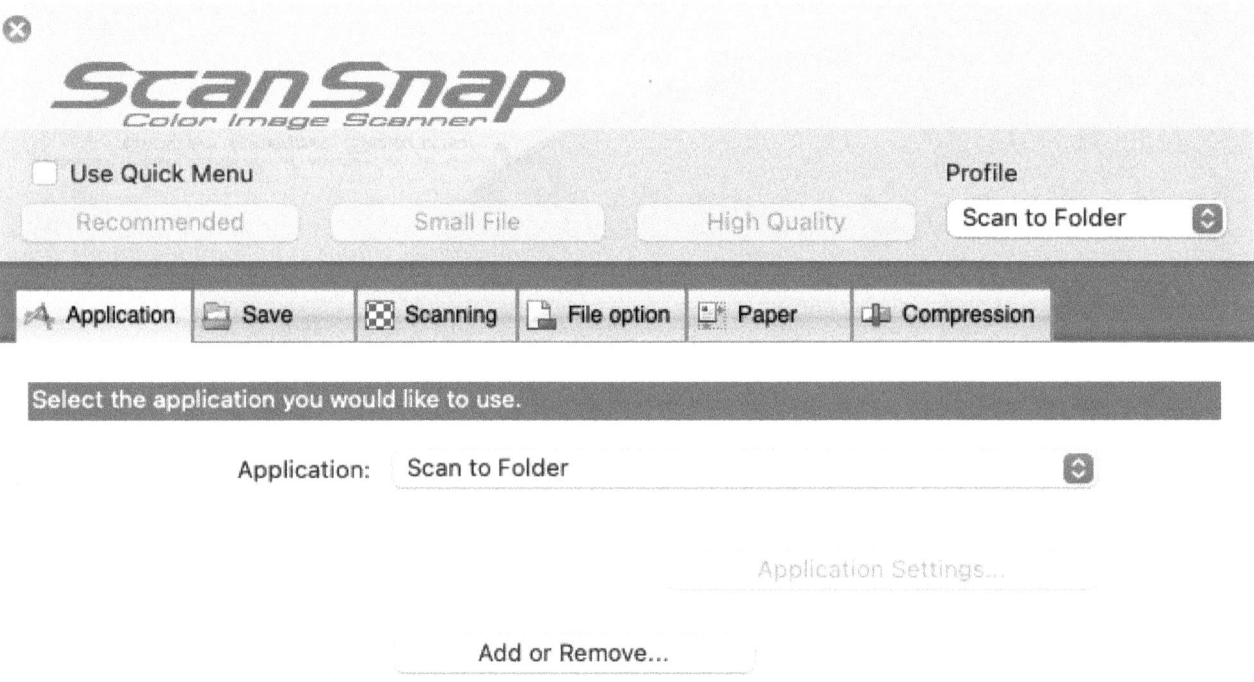

Step 2: Save

Set up the scanner to save directly into the "_attachments" folder. This folder should have been made in the Obsidian Vault.

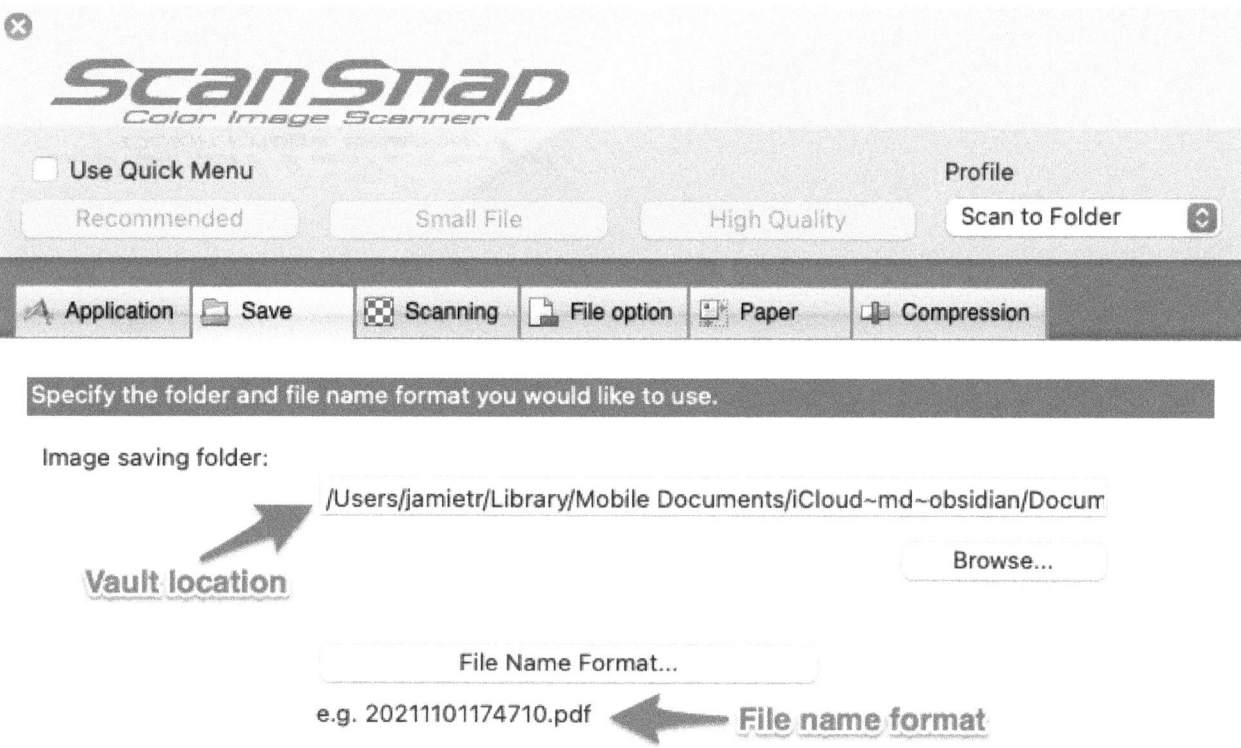

Then choose the file name format, and choose the YYYYmmddhhmmss format. Zettelkasten format is mostly perfect for prefixing note names. If you often conduct date searches or think date searches are the best fit to identify your raw file in Obsidian, then you might have to take this route.

Step 3: Choose file options

Note: the scanner automatically sets the file format to PDF, but you can choose a preferred file option in the file format section. Select the convert to searchable PDF checklist.

Currently, Obsidian does not support PDF search, but it is possible to get that update very soon, at least as a Community Plug-in, even though not in the core plug-in section.

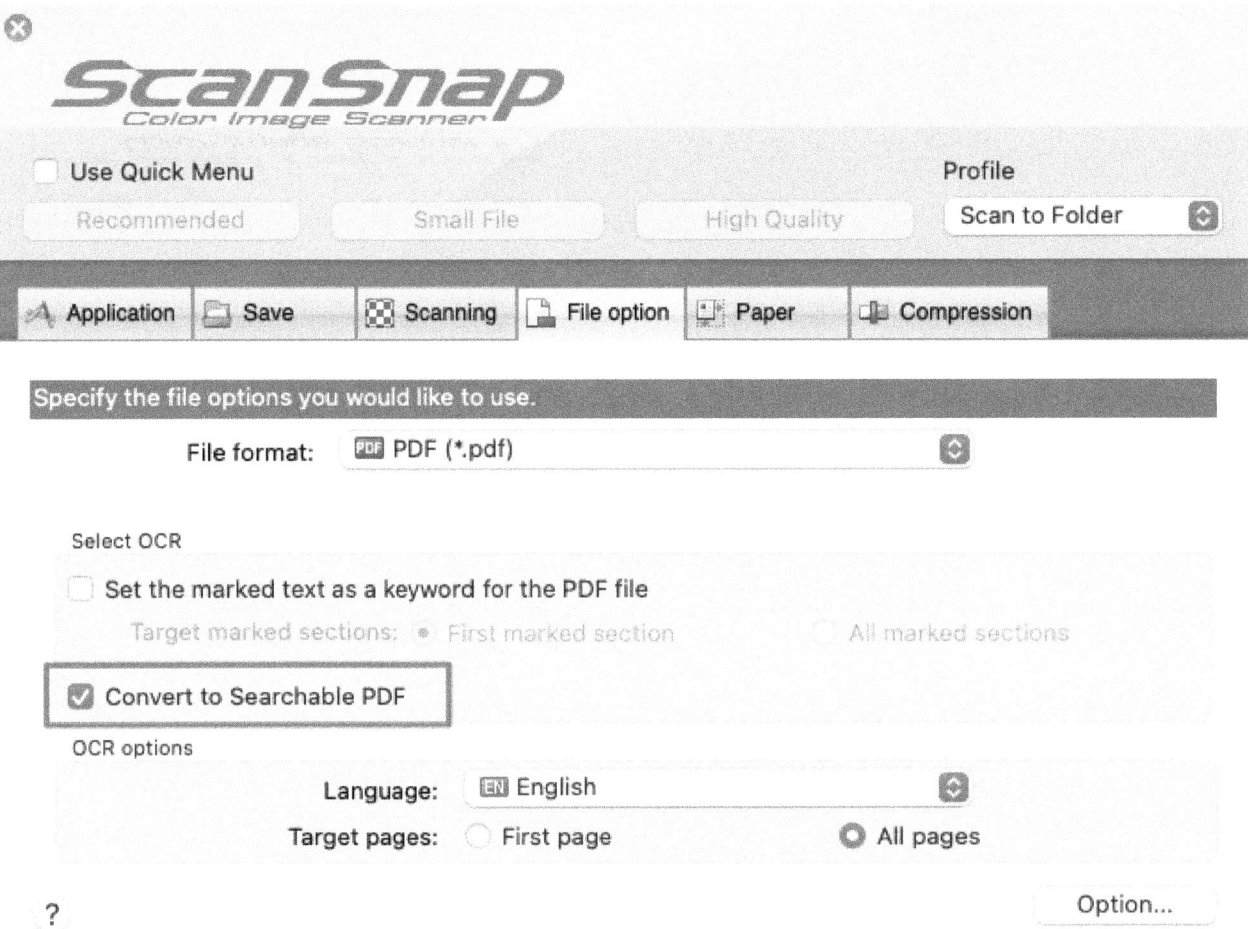

After making these adjustments, set up the document on the scanner and push the blue scan button to scan it into Obsidian. The PDF file is automatically saved in the _attachments folder in my Vault after the document has been scanned.

Step 4: Making a Note on the PDF

At this point, you can:

Give the PDF a practical name that you easily locate in the Vault.

To "contain" the PDF, you can make a structured note in Obsidian. This is so you can link the note with the PDF by using the metadata (tags, etc.) in the note. That makes it simple to refer to the document with the prepared note containing a transcluded note link to the PDF file.

Below is Jamie Todd's Covid-19 immunization card. The file house a structured note linked to the scanned PDF. However, in the screenshot is how the PDF shows in both preview and edit modes:

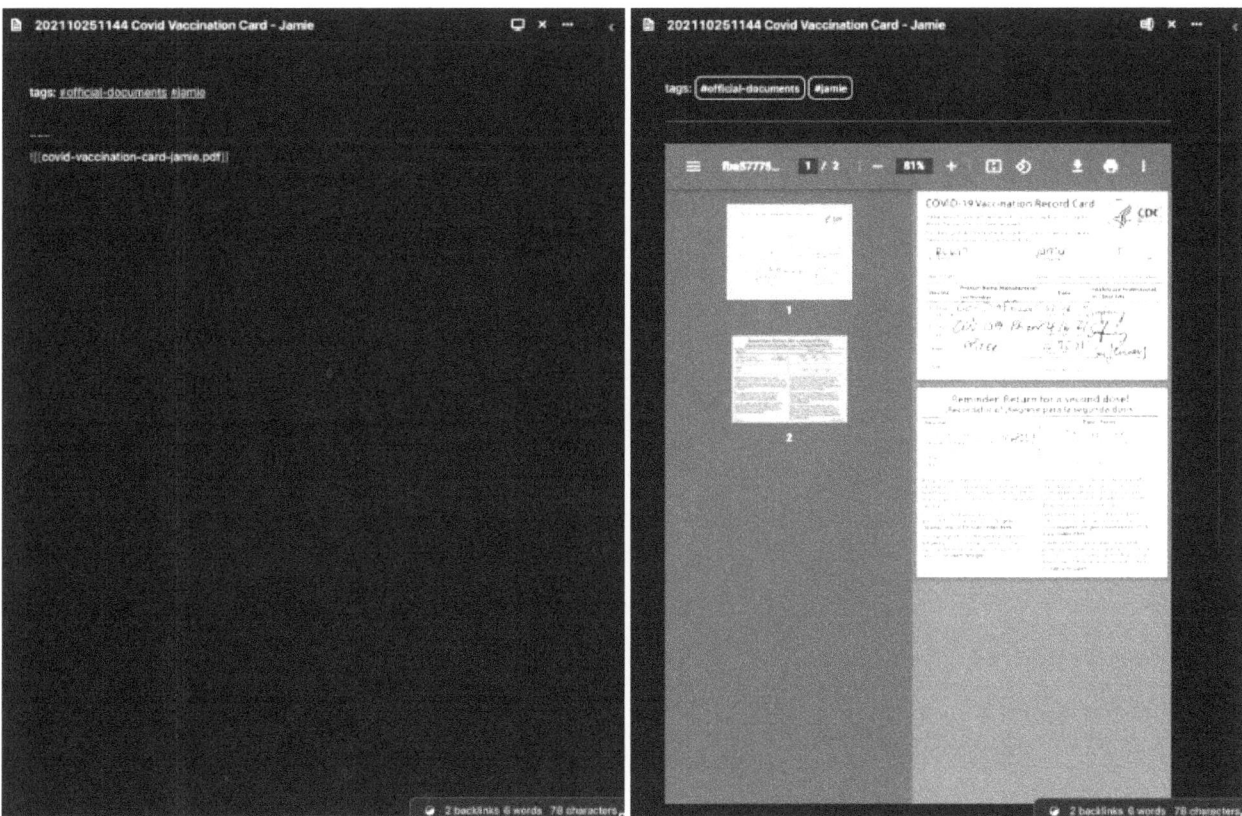

Including the scanned paper in a structured note may seem unnecessary, but by doing so, you can add tags and other components to the document that you couldn't add to a basic PDF.

How to Secure your Ideas and Notes in Obsidian

While working with data, security is an essential factor to consider. And to this effect, we will work with an onion layer approach to securing your Obsidian files. However, just every pro has a con; each technique by itself is not ideal. But when taken together, they surely will give a high sense of security and comfort sufficient to not worry about anything.

On that note, we will express these layers of data security in Obsidian: data encryption, digital access, and physical access. The diagram below shows a system of how the onion data security approach looks like. However, we will like to start with physical access.

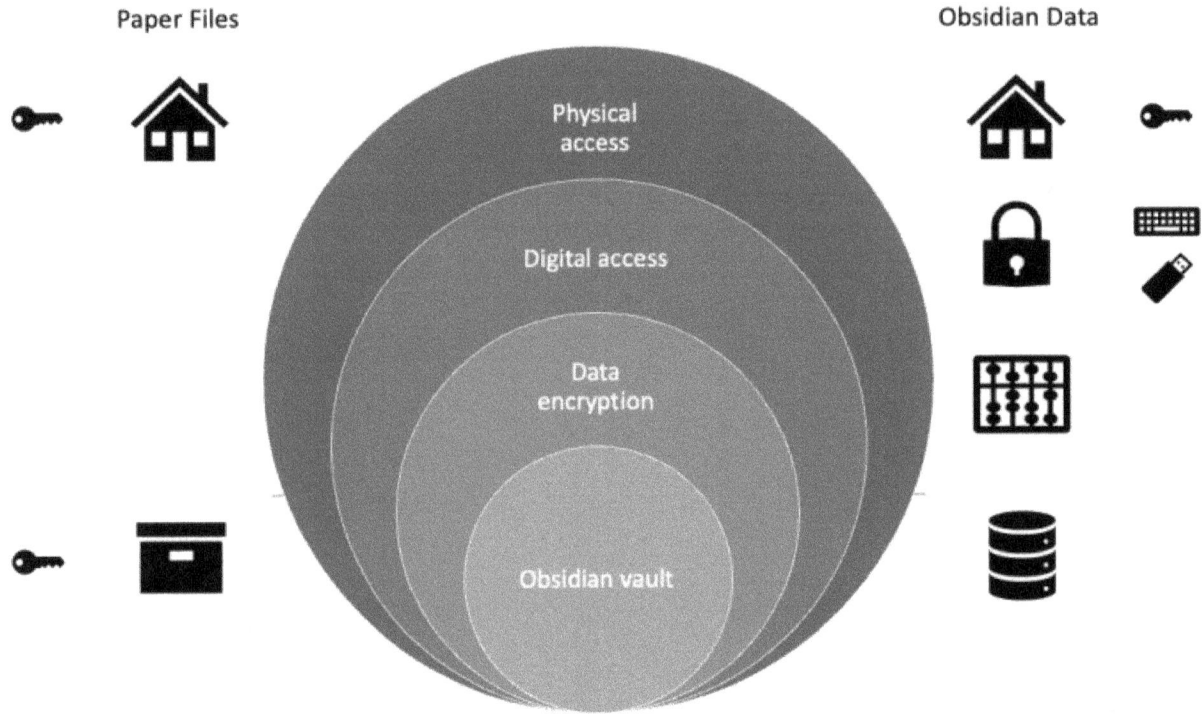

Securing physical data access on Obsidian

One of its main selling points is that data is stored locally by default in Obsidian. That means that you have all your notes perfectly stored on your laptop, desktop or mobile in your office or house.

If someone needs access to your computer, they also need access to your office or your phone; they will need to enter your house first or office first. And that is with your physical permission. The "physical access" layer in the graphic above serves as an illustration of this. The residence on the right side stands in for physical access to your Obsidian data.

Physical access to your notes is currently the same in both situations. To get to your laptop or phone, someone needs to get access from you. However, it is important to note that you occasionally overhear arguments against the digital storage of particular sorts of data. This makes complete sense. Everyone must establish their level of comfort. However, locally stored data are almost identical to taking your note on a jotter because you are 100% in control of the security (physical security).

There may be several layers of physical security in and of itself.

1. Create a highly inaccessible lock to the office door
2. Install a good lock for the house door
3. For extra security set up and alarm system (All this for sensitive information).

Long before Obsidian, when most people's files were on paper and kept in a filing cabinet, most people didn't have to worry about data security. That makes Obsidian one of the best options because your data is stored locally on your computer. This approach has almost the same level of security as the physical type.

Securing digital data access on Obsidian

But suppose someone could get past the physical security barrier and take a seat in front of a computer or flash drive where the Vault is stored. Digital access to your Obsidian data would be protected by the second layer of the onion, which goes on now.

A person would first need to be able to sign into the flash drive using a password that has access to the Vault to access the Obsidian notes. That essentially means that a password is required to sign into a computer. It is best to have a unique password for each account. One password can only be used to access one particular device or service. For easy remembrance, you can use a password manager or just try long-form passwords with a combination of numbers, signs and alphabets.

For our exercise, let's assume that the intruder manages to crack your computer's password, which is complicated and one-of-a-kind. Then what? Digital access can include various components, just like physical access can (keys, alarms, etc.). For best practice, initiate a two-factor authentication in addition to a strong, one-time password. It takes more than a password to access the computer. It's necessary to use the second type of verification. Multi-factor authentication can take many forms, including biometrics, authenticator tools, text messages to other devices, and wholly distinct devices like YubiKeys.

It really isn't worth worrying about if someone manages to bypass the two-factor authentication, compromise my physical security, and figure out the password. Imagine, for example; you're your notes were kept on paper and kept in a jotter, as shown in the image to the left. The security onion's digital access layer is absent in this situation. So, let's compare what it takes to retrieve your notes in Obsidian in the case and on paper:

Location	Paper	Obsidian
Physical	1. House access (key, alarm code, etc.) 2. Entry to the office 3. Use of the jotter (key?)	1. House access (key, alarm code, etc.) 2. Office accessibility
Digital	None	1. Be aware of the complex password system. 2. Gain access to your backup authentication method

Accessing your data would be simpler if it were kept on paper in your workplace rather than in Obsidian, with the Vault kept locally on your computer.

Data encoding

Suppose our irate villain decides to simply take my computer with them after successfully entering your workplace but fails to get beyond the machine's digital protection to access the data on the hard drive, possibly by mounting it on another device. The situation is starting to sound ridiculous, but let's stick with it.

You can encrypt your hard drive with FileVault. If you have any, it comes inbuilt on MasOS, with a 256-bit key and 128-bit AES encryption. Until the appropriate authorization has been granted, the data on the disk is encrypted at rest; after that, the data is decrypted. In this context, "proper authorization" refers to the access called for in paragraph 2 above. There is no realistic way to decrypt the data without a password and legitimate authentication from a different authenticator. The computer would be useless to whoever has it until they erased the drive, in which case they would no longer have access to the data.

Together, these three onion layers form the whole. If you can initiate all three processes, it is obvious that you can see a level of comfort while you focus on creating high-value notes. Although there is a chance of a breach, it is so unlikely that you don't need to worry.

Notes syncing and cloud security

Ah, but what if I want to use different devices to access my notes?

Is there a chance that someone could access my cloud-based data?

Your best option is to synchronize your files and notes. That will comfortably give you access to different devices.

For optimal performance, it will be best to use the Sync service offered by Obsidian. You can simply set up a quick, dependable sync service and never have to fiddle with it again.

Obsidian Sync has two encryption models:

- Controlled encryption
- End-to-end encryption.

It will be best to use end-to-end encryption because it gives perfect anonymity. For this, data is encrypted before it is transported to and from Obsidian's sync service, even if it is already encrypted on your hard drive. On Obsidian servers, it is also encrypted. The best part is that you have access to the data. The encryption password is unknown to anyone, even the developers. However, the con is that you wouldn't be able to access the Vault in the Obsidian Sync service if you ever forgot your password.

Even if the data is kept in Obsidian Sync, the three layers of my security onion still hold. Physical access to the server hosting the data would be required. They would require a password to decrypt the server's data and digital access to that data.

How to secure Obsidian on mobile devices

Mobile devices are the most venerable amongst all the security access points, especially for physical security, because it is very easy to lose them. You might forget at a spot, or it might even be stolen without you knowing.

But even at that, it is at this point that we can employ the other layers. For someone to access your phone data, they generally need direct access. Additionally, direct access to solid-state storage is useless because data on iPhones is encrypted. In addition, your phone is secured so that after a specific number of unsuccessful attempts to sign in, the phone will wipe its data, rendering it worthless to anyone looking for it. If you find the phone missing and it is turned on and can contact a cellular network, you can also delete the data remotely.

Extra Safety Tips

Data protection involves more than just limiting illegal access. Additionally, it guarantees that you will have access when you need it. Here are some more measures you take to safeguard your vital information (including the Obsidian Vault).

Try VPN

It is important to always be security conscious; it is not enough to assume that no one is watching. So, while on private or public WIFI, make sure to use a VPN when you have vital information on your phone to ensure data protection. By doing this, you can stop worrying about someone spying on your network without your knowledge. Thanks to the VPN service, the data is protected end-to-end from when it leaves your device.

Data Archiving

This involves backing up your details often. Not just on your devices but also on the cloud. You will need to continuously back up your data on your computers. Timemachine might be a nice option to save on an external disk, so you can restore quickly in case of any lags or errors.

Best Practices

Just as best practices are important for success while using any system, it is also important to practice some of the ideas below if you really want to get the best out of your "**Second Brain**":

Record Often

The more the note, the easier it is. So the key to success while using an Obsidian is in the volume. We create ideas there don't just fly in from the blues. That said, your Obsidian becomes more helpful as the quantity and connections of your notes grow. So to effectively leverage the power of your second brain, recording as often as possible is important.

Review meticulously

Check for "unlinked mentions." You might have accidentally mentioned existing notes that you have not yet connected to or investigated as your repository of notes grows. However, the Obsidian algorithm classifies them as unlinked mentions. You can stay on top of this and make sure you don't miss that "Aha" moment by scheduling a search of "unlinked mentions."

Activate the "random note" function by clicking the dice icon on the left toolbar. That produces random tones. This pushes you to think back on long-forgotten concepts and inspires chance discovery.

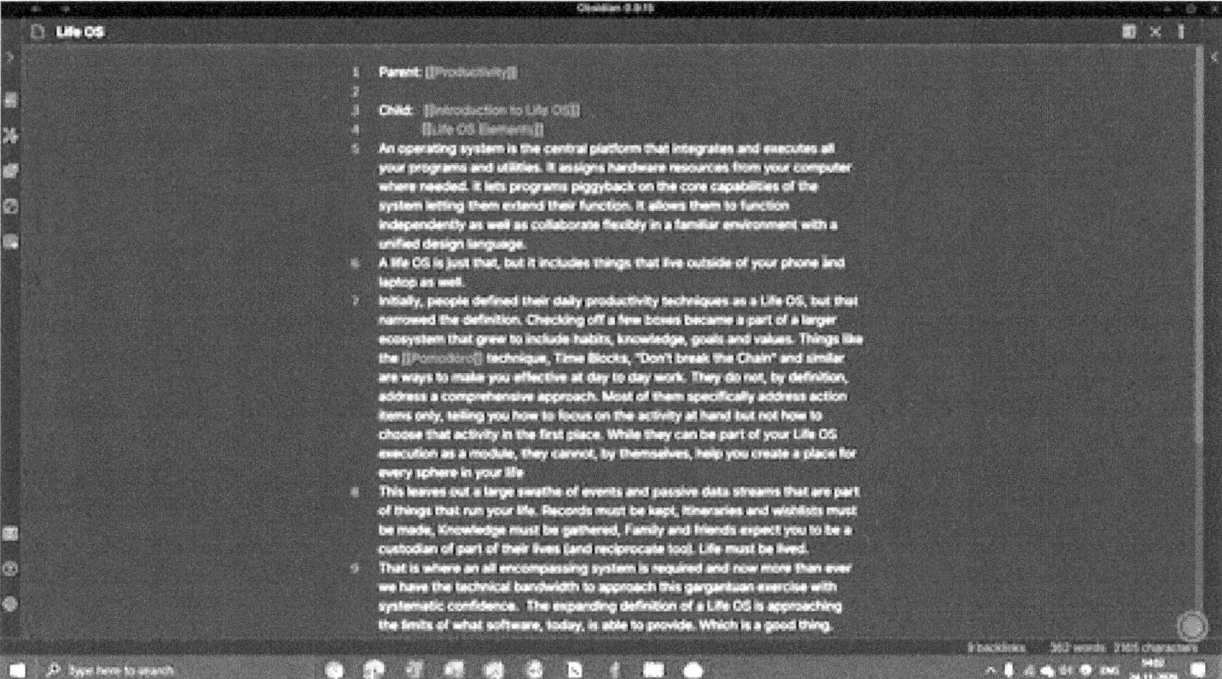

Conclusion

Understanding and leveraging the power of Obsidian is a very vital essence of this piece, and quite obviously, it is an amazing tool to help create a good connection between ideas as you practically implement them.

Now that you are aware of what Obsidian is, you can see why you might want to use it to create your library of related ideas as you are more familiar with the user interface now familiar. Additionally, you know how to take your first note and establish your first few contacts.

Obsidian is no longer a mystery to you at this point. You now have everything needed to rule the world today with your public second brain, completely free. All that's left is you implement these processes in your daily leaving, and you are off to the moon; that all depends on you and how you synchronize your routine with the Obsidian App to help anytime.

www.ingramcontent.com/pod-product-compliance
Lightning Source LLC
LaVergne TN
LVHW070215080526
838202LV00067B/6829